The
Mom
Ministry

Lisa Hartell

The Mom Ministry

ISBN 0-9749234-0-0

All Scripture quotations, unless otherwise indicated, are from the New International Version.   Copyright 1983, B. B. Kirkbride Bible Company, Inc.

King James Version, Copyright 1998, Zondervan Publishing House.

Amplified Version, Copyright 1987, Zondervan Publishing House.

Though at times it may be grammatically incorrect, throughout this printing, we have deliberately refrained from capitalizing the name of satan to refrain from honoring him in any way.

Printed in the United States by Morris Publishing
3212 East Highway 30
Kearney, NE 68847
1-800-650-7888

This book is lovingly dedicated
In memory of

My Dearest Mother,
Irene Piotrowski
Who went home to heaven, 9-17-2001

and My Big Sister in Christ,
Wendy Mogle
Who went home to heaven, 4-29-2003

God used them as Mom's who ministered to me
to sow eternal seeds in my life.

They continue to inspire me…
to pray and seek Jesus like never before,
and to raise my children to do the same.

Their legacies speak, today…
with His Divine, Eternal Voice

CONTENTS

Modern Motherhood ~ We Must Be Led by the Holy
Spirit ~ All Things are Possible ~ Leading The Leaders ~
How Far Will You Go? ~ Freedom To Be The Real You

Are Our Families Ready? ~ God Has a Message For You
~ Isaiah 61 ~ Change Is Coming ~ Think Of It Like This ~
Change Your Talk And It Will Change Your Walk

I See A Dove ~ What Does It All Mean ~ There's More ~
Want It. Pray It. See It Happen. ~ The Burden ~ The Dove
Makes All The Difference ~ Lift Your Eyes – Look For The
Dove ~ The Dove ~ A Faith of Their Own

Eureka ~ Look For God's Purpose – Listen For God's
Voice - In Every Circumstance ~ Turning Points ~ Prayer
~ Am I Willing? ~ It's Not About Perfection ~ Proverbs of
The Mom Ministry

Acknowledgements

Jesus – THANK YOU is not a big enough word. I'll never forget the moment you came, opened the jail cell door, turned the key, and said, "it's ok, Lisa, you can come out now, you're free…" Thanks, My Heavenly Father, for making your self so real to me, for being so faithful and for helping me obey, when I knew in my own strength, I couldn't. You enabled me to step out by faith, every time, in your grace. You truly are the True and Perfect Prodigal Father. I stand in "awe" of You. Holy Spirit, Your presence is the ultimate! You are the Sweetest.   I honor you and I'm not going anywhere WITHOUT YOU!

Andy – My best earthly friend in the world, next to the Lord… Thank you, just doesn't seem to be enough - for your selfless love, and always encouraging me to obey God wholeheartedly. I'm so blessed that God chose us, together. This book wouldn't be in print if it weren't for you. Your love, time, and self-sacrifice are immeasurable. You are truly a valiant man of God with a servant's heart. I am so proud to stand at your side, as 'one' in Him…

Andrew and AJ – You are like the icing on my cake. When God put it in my heart to pray for two boys, I could never have imagined receiving all that I have through your lives and hearts. You are the world's best sons…you make me laugh and have been God's greatest instruments in molding my heart to become more and more like Jesus. I am humbled to be chosen by the Lord to minister to you. As I grow in Jesus, your love and tender hearts are His vessels to speak to me so often. Out of the mouth of babes, God perfects praise… Andrew, the night before I began to write this book, God put a "word" in your mouth to carry me through, to see the delivery of this "baby". Truly, He has already begun to use you in MIGHTY ways – and this is only the beginning for you. AJ, you lost your first tooth, on the Eve of this book's beginning. Every time you've lisped, it has brought a smile to my face, and along with it strength, to rub my tired eyes and begin to write again. You have been my encouragers and instruments of God's great grace. For the past twelve years, God has used you to open my eyes to "*The Mom Ministry*". God's plan for your life is MIGHTY! This book is our family's "baby" – thanks for doing your part on the team - for allowing God to use you and me to build up the body of Christ. Your reward is rich in heaven.

My family – We were given one of the greatest earthly gifts, to have a Mom that knew her most important work was prayer. Today, we are walking in some of the many blessings that she prayed for us. And the best is yet to come! As she took her last step and started to cross over the threshold into eternity, she was able to turn around, look back at us and smile (knowing that her work was finished). Ours has just begun. May God find us faithful! For in those moments, I believe the Lord assured her that her every prayer was answered...for you and for me. What could we give our children that is more valuable than that? She showed us the reality of a deep relationship with a loving and Almighty God. May we continue to grow as a family in understanding of what that truly means. I love you, and consider each of you a priceless gift from God.

I want to thank Linda Molenda and sweet "Betty-Betty" (Betty Biernat) in a special way for your hours of prayer coverage on each page of this book. No one but the Lord knows how much you have contributed in sacrifice, love, and faithfulness to Him in this – these pages are in print, because of you, too! God's grace even covers huge editing jobs! Truly we partner in the joys of the harvest! His Spirit accomplishes miracles through you! I am grateful to God for our "sisterhood"!

To Ann, Ron, Denise, Danielle, and our precious family (the Kingdom of God), for your intercession, support, and anointed words of encouragement – THANK YOU and God Bless You RICHLY! It's Jesus IN you, the hope of glory, who speaks to me in countless ways. You are each a gift to us, and RICHLY anointed with His presence.

In great love and gratitude, I want to say thank you to the many spiritual leaders who have poured into the lives of our family. Some of the countless holy seeds you've sown have begun to come to fruition in the Kingdom, our prayer is that many more of those seeds will be multiplied through the pages of the book you now hold in your hands. God's plan is far bigger than we can imagine ~ it's all about Him and moving in His Spirit to reach the lost, broken, captive, and hurting with the Good News. There is a heavenly treasure within you that shines as brightly as the sun, and it's JESUS. HE IS our treasure who is divinely connecting all the dots of His Great and Mighty Plan! As a family, we thank you for exemplifying lives that are sold out to going all the way with Christ Jesus! We love you! Even more... Your Heavenly Father does! Your reward is great in heaven!

Introduction

Before I delve into this exciting topic of "*The Mom Ministry*", I want to begin by stating my purpose for writing this book. It's truly an act of obedience to the voice of the Holy Spirit. As I write, my heart is yearning to have the Lord unfold more of His purpose and will for my own life through this adventure called, "*The Mom Ministry*".

When the Lord first instructed me to write this, His direction was perfectly clear. At first, because of my own feelings of inadequacy, I didn't take the Lord very seriously. Like Moses, I found myself continuously dismissing it from my mind as, "an unlikely project". But God is faithful to not give up on sending His message to each of us, isn't He? He gently but persistently tugs at our hearts about it until we finally get the message and obey. And for that I am so grateful!

I thank God for the thousands of answered prayers, and for the clear direction to begin. When we step out in faith, He meets us on the water. After a time of wrestling and trying to convince my husband and the Lord that there must be some other person to do this, I went into a season of focused prayer and then sat down and began to peck away at the keyboard. God had given me a new resolve. First, that God doesn't call the equipped He equips the called. Second, this is about walking on the edge, believing that He has gone out before me to speak to those who are hungering and crying out for help. Are you one of those I'm speaking of today?

If you are, I have good news for you. Jesus is waiting to meet you where you are. To those who are genuinely hungering to be molded into the image of Christ in their motherhood and ministry – He sees your heart. He will lead you one revelation at a time. For those who feel such lack and inability within themselves, He longs to use and bless you, to assure you that He truly enables the willing and obedient. If you happen to be one that has found yourself swimming in the cesspool of your own failures, know this: God's not mad at you. He's eagerly waiting to show you His mercy, comfort, and forgiveness…to release you from the weight of it all - today!

Jesus desires to be the source of inspiration and strength in you, not just for your benefit, but for your children, for your grandchildren, and for the many more that will be touched, changed, and empowered by Him, through you.

More and more I see and hear the struggles of women trying to keep it all together. Who would argue that we live in the "busiest" generation in history? To try to make light of our lives being so busy, comedians joke that Mom's today battle with "ADD" (Attention Deficit Disorder). During serious moments of sharing heart to heart, I've listened to women speak of their struggles with juggling all the many hats we have to wear. They wrestle with guilt at the end of the day for not spending enough time with their children (who are the very ones they are working so hard to raise). Quiet moments of relaxation often lead to sobering thoughts that "quality-time" seems to be slipping away more and more. This often leaves us feeling defeated.

My only claim today, is that God has called me to be a clay vessel to shout from the housetops what He has whispered to my heart. My desire is to see His heart and thoughts touch yours (not with mesmerizing eloquence or clever terminology, but with simplicity, truth, grace, and His anointing). For that's what makes the difference and brings lasting changes of beauty. It's Jesus alone that can liberate us to run the race, and after falling, grant us the mercy and amazing grace to get up one more time and dare to run again until we finish the race.

We in ourselves don't have the ability to bring eternal change or fulfill this awesome purpose that God has for us. To a certain degree we do have the ability to change some things about our personalities and habits, but to actually affect the spirit and direction of our entire life and children?

We make the decision to turn and obey, but GOD ultimately supplies all the power and transforming work as we yield to His daily plan for our lives.

I have a God-given desire to see the Lord illuminate this ministry to my own heart every day. My prayer of faith is that through the pages of this book and His Holy Word, you and I will walk together and find ourselves enjoying a "journey of discovery." To discover and unlock all that God has implanted deep within us.

We'll talk about what God really intends for the Mom's of today. We'll look ahead and dream, taking the limits off of what we once thought God could do through us, and allow Him to expand our vision for our own lives and destiny. We'll take scripture, study it, and learn to apply it in ways that work, today – ways that set us free – and ways that will touch and change the lives of our family and world. And through it all, we will ask God to take us deeper in Him.

I believe, you too, will discover more and more as you read. I encourage you to take the time as you read to pause, think and pray about how these things apply to you and your children.

It's a good idea to journal as many of your discoveries, as possible. It is as you study God's word, pray, and write that the Holy Spirit will meet you and reveal even MORE to your heart. Journaling will also serve as a permanent record of God's molding and shaping your heart. He will prove Himself to be more real than what you see with your eyes. Later, it will serve as a treasured inheritance for your children and grandchildren.

For an added aid, keep *The Mom Ministry Prayer Journal* handy as you read. *The Children's Prayer Journal* can be used to introduce your children to the countless and lasting benefits of journaling. I encourage you to use your journal to record key scriptures and prayers that the Holy Spirit impresses upon your heart. Include areas of special prayer you want to remember each day, and areas that you want to see God change in the lives of you and your children.

I urge you today, before you "dive in" to your *Mom Ministry*, to get ready to give up, and just "let God have His

way". To those who have already done so, and find
yourselves back in the same boat once again - get ready to
give it up to God AGAIN, and AGAIN, and AGAIN...until you
find yourself getting used to "letting Him do all the driving".

Lesson #1 in *The Mom Ministry* is:

"We let God do all the driving –
only then, can we enjoy
the beautiful scenery along the way".

one

What Is
The Mom Ministry?

hen the Lord first directed me to write this, I thought, "*The Mom Ministry*? Is there such a thing?" For many months, this phrase returned to my mind. In prayer one day, I asked Him about it, "Lord, how can I write a book about a ministry that I've never heard of before"?

In the days ahead, the Lord began to unveil truths in my heart. As I prayed and walked by faith, He unfolded more and more of His vision for "*The Mom*

Ministry." As we step out in obedience to His voice, we find the road comes alive with discovering deeper truths and revelation in God's ways and word. God's journey for us is designed and orchestrated so that each time we do, He reveals more of Himself to us ~ and we are forever changed. I keep a little phrase the Lord spoke to me long ago near my writing desk, it says very simply,

~ Jesus ~

The more we spend time with Him,
the more we know Him.
The more we know Him, the more we love Him.
The more we love Him, the more we obey Him.
The more we obey Him...
the more LIKE HIM we become."

Our path of obedience with Him requires faith and courage to move forward. It leads us into greater levels of freedom and conforms us more into His image. Each step of obedience activates the release of my own faith and it's growth. Our understanding of Him, His love, and His holiness expands with every step.

Today, as you and I walk together, through the pages of this book, I am truly expecting His anointing to flow into the areas of your life as a woman of God and a mother, that have previously held you back. My prayer is that as I share my heart, you'll be encouraged and forever changed. I believe in divine appointments that are ordained by God to usher us into new truths. God uses them to move us forward into His plan for our lives.

I believe God planned for you and I to sit down and journey together today. Sound too dreamy? Dare to believe it. We've had many divine appointments in our personal walks with the Lord. God uses many ways to speak to us: His word, prayer, music, people, children, situations, church services, nature, art, tapes and yes, even books. The Holy Spirit is ready and willing to ignite your heart with light and truth that will bring new freedom to your heart and mind.

As you read today, expect God to touch and change your heart, making it more like His own.

MODERN MOTHERHOOD

God's instruction to write this book, provoked me to think long and hard about what being a Mom really means today? Our world has changed in so many ways since the 1920's when my Mom was raised. Technology, Nintendo, internet connections, computers, palm pilots, day planners, cell phones, and organizers are all part of our every day lives.

Sometimes we think, "STOP! Where can we get off? There's just too much to keep track of." This is usually just before we begin thinking about our next vacation. Though we know that culturally, "Motherhood" has changed quite a bit, our emotional, spiritual, and physical needs remain the same.

When we have half a minute to take notice of what's really going on around us, we see that being a Mom is more than accomplishing the impossible feat of working hard, washing clothes, driving "Mom's Taxi" all over town, dropping off Bobby's lunch at school, making stops at soccer games, and hurrying to the next birthday party. Motherhood is more than keeping food on the table, wearing 12 hats and being the "Jack of all trades". It's more than making it through the daily struggle of discovering where the next meal is going to come from.

Deep inside us, is a God-implanted question that yearns to know, "What is my real PURPOSE in all of this?" Have you ever wondered, "Am I really making a difference in my children?" "Why do I keep doing the same things my Mom did?" And some days we may ask, "Lord, am I raising or wrecking, my kids"? How do we balance it all and accomplish all that we are supposed to?

Yes, times have changed, indeed. Harry Potter's witchcraft and New Age teaching have hit our schools with full force. Books that teach our children how to cast spells and read Tara cards are sold by the thousands each week. One might ask, "how do you NOT get overwhelmed by all of this and continue to train up our children in the way they should go, in the midst of such a worldly society"?

WE MUST BE LED BY
THE HOLY SPIRIT

God has a plan and a way of escape for our societies that are filled with busy Moms. Using the keys of wisdom and walking in obedience to the Word of God is part of it. But there's more. The Bible speaks of David's mighty men coming alongside him for battle. This holds a timely and priceless message for each of us today. I remember learning a great lesson through one of these tribes, called the Tribe of Issachar. 1 Chronicles 12:32 says that the Tribe of Issachar,

**"had understanding of the times
to know what Israel ought to do."
(Amplified Version)**

Like the Tribe of Issachar, it is imperative that we do two things: 1) know the times and what we should do, and 2) teach our children to do the same. We find ourselves desperately in need of that level of understanding today. In the midst of all our responsibilities, how can each of us know the spiritual times and know what we ought to do "with" and "for" our children? Where can we find such revelation and wisdom?

Whether you are a new Christian, just starting out on your journey of faith, or a seasoned woman of God that knows the heat of the fires of testing, God has a fresh message for you concerning being an anointed minister to children. The Bible tells us that the word of God and the Holy Spirit are given to us for this reason. God's word says the following things about wisdom and the Fear of the Lord.

*"...for giving prudence to the simple,
knowledge and discretion to the young –
let the wise listen and add to their learning, and let the
discerning get guidance - for understanding proverbs
and parables, the sayings and riddles of the wise.
The Fear of the Lord is the beginning of knowledge, but
fools despise wisdom and discipline."*
Proverbs 1:4-7

"The Fear of the Lord is the beginning of wisdom, and knowledge of Him is understanding." If we are going to be empowered by His spirit and fulfill all God's desires for us, we are going to have to wake up to the reality of the times and seasons we live in. Like the Tribe of Issachar, we must seek the Lord to know the times and know what we should do.

Many prayer partners have been interceding that as you read the pages of this book, the Lord will speak to you and strengthen you. By way of the Holy Spirit, I believe that He is going to impart in you, understanding and revelation to know the times and your purpose as a Mom in this new millennium. In addition to that, I am believing that as you read and continue to seek Him with all of your heart, He is going to empower you to do the things you once thought were impossible.

ALL THINGS ARE POSSIBLE

By faith, I believe God is going to awaken your dreams, gifts, and destiny, and activate the sleeping giant within you. The Holy Spirit's anointing is available to break yokes of bondage off of your life to see you set free to be all that God has called you to be.

There is a generation of children, teens, and young adults that are destined for greatness and need to be trained. They are in desperate need of their activation and release in the Kingdom of God! Our Pastors, Children's Workers, and Sunday School Teachers can't do it alone. The job is too big! This generation has been called by God to change the world and do their part in the fullness of the harvest. They are a generation that is carrying within them the ability to release the Kingdom of God and His will in the earth like we've never seen or imagined before.

LEADING THE LEADERS

When God gets ready to raise up young leaders, He begins to work in and mold the hearts of their spiritual mothers. It takes spiritual mothers to train up and raise spiritual leaders. God has given us the keys of the Kingdom. The Spirit of God through Mothers, can turn the heart of a nation back to God, build His Kingdom, and in essence impact the world. Being a spiritual mother is not limited to your blood descendents. They can be your adopted children, or special children that God brings you to mentor in your neighborhood, church, or other organization.

Remember Timothy? Paul acknowledged his training in the faith by his mother and grandmother. For added study, read the stories of the Mothers of Moses, Samuel, John the Baptist, and Jesus. Each of these mothers were completely devoted to and led by the Spirit of God.

HOW FAR WILL YOU GO?

In order to take the plunge in *The Mom Ministry*, each of us must first ask ourselves two soul-searching questions:

1) Are you willing to go all the way and let God change your own heart? For it is out

of a pure heart that the Kingdom of God goes forth?

2) Do you truly believe all of God's word? Fear, doubt, and unbelief are the enemies of your mind, body, and spirit. In a later chapter, we will take the time to study how to walk in victory to overcome these in our ministry as Moms.

As we move through the pages of *The Mom Ministry*, let the Holy Spirit remove the limitations that you've been handed along the way. Such as the ones that you may have been born with, including: the mindsets that lock us into thinking and saying, "I can't", "I'm not enough", "I'll never change", "it's just too hard", or "I've failed too many times".

"*The Mom Ministry*" is about liberation. Liberation for a generation of Moms that are called to raise up perhaps the most earth-shaking generation in history. The generation that is sent into our schools and world like David, Samuel, and Joshua, who hear from God and are radically obedient to do whatever He says.

Are you ready? If so, I encourage you to take a moment and sincerely pray the following prayer with me. Let's start our journey by coming into agreement with God's word so that His will can be established in every area of your life and *Mom Ministry*.

**Father in heaven,
humbly we come before you in agreement,
and in the matchless name of Jesus. We boldly come
before your throne of grace to receive mercy.
Covered in the shed blood of Jesus, we ask you, Lord,
to send your Holy Spirit, to minister to me,**

the grace, truth, and understanding
that leads to wisdom
and liberty in my mind, body, and spirit.
I ask you to set me free to be all that you have
destined me to be. First, as your daughter,
Second, as a Woman of God,
and Third, as a Mother.
I open my heart to what your Spirit
is saying to me, Lord.
I ask that you restore
my heart, mind, time, and family.
Help me see the ministry of being an anointed Mom
the way that you do. I ask that you breath on me the
breath of LIFE that liberates me from everything that
holds me back and blinds me. Take your Holy Word,
the Sword of the Spirit, and cut to the very root of the
things that are in my heart, that stop me from growing
and moving in you,
and being transformed by your Spirit.
Liberate me from the mindsets
that hinder me from changing and
believing that through YOU, I CAN do ALL things. In
Jesus' Name, we believe that we receive what we
have asked for and we refuse to doubt!
I will give you all the
praise, honor, and glory, you are so deserving of.
Thank You, Father.   Amen.

FREEDOM TO BE THE
REAL YOU

By trusting in the work of the blood of Jesus that
was shed for us on the cross, we are free to rely on the

Holy Spirit's power and strength to minister to our children with God's heart. *The Mom Ministry* cannot be accomplished apart from an intimate relationship with the Father, Son, and Holy Spirit. It's about receiving a revelation of what the Holy Spirit is saying to you about the value and importance of who you really are in Christ. What God has for you to accomplish as you minister to your children in the home is eternal. It will be used to build the Kingdom of God.

The Mom Ministry is a work of the Spirit that can only be done by God *through* us. Sound too spiritual for you? Just hold on for the ride, it's actually the most freeing and exciting journey in all the world.

In addition to your sacrifice, It's your road to a new level of peace and enjoyment in raising your children. It's a road that leads to blessings, answered prayers, and the impossibilities becoming POSSIBLE.

World re-known evangelist, Louis Palau, once said, that his whole ministry was transformed when a shift took place in his own thinking.
He writes,

**"The whole thing is 'not I, but Christ in me.'
It's not what I'm going to do <u>for</u> you but rather
what You are going to do <u>through</u> me."**[1]

It was this very realization that changed his focus. We become wearied when we fight and struggle to persevere in our own strength.

There is a sense of hopelessness when you know you're looking in the right place and still not finding the answer. Have you ever wanted to throw your hands up in the air and say, "forget it, God...I just don't understand what I'm doing wrong, and why it is such a struggle?" Though we have the Word, Christian conferences, and knowledge, who hasn't had days, weeks, or even years of feeling utterly defeated?

It's time to shift our focus from our daily distractions to God's divine purpose in our motherhood. It's time to let Him make us His anointed ministers in our home – so that He can do *through* us, what only He can do.

two

Isaiah 61
The Time Is Now

I believe we have crossed a threshold in the Spirit. By that I mean, we are standing at the door of the return of Christ and have stepped into the greatest spiritual battle the earth has ever seen. Scripture is clear that before the return of Christ, we would see cataclysmic changes both upon the earth and in the heavens. All of these point to His eminent return, being close at hand.

In fact, I had a dream not long ago that we, the church, were not only aware that the day of Jesus' return was close, but that we were expecting Him at any moment!

We were all scurrying around to help one another get dressed. There was much joy among God's people as I ran around helping my brothers and sisters get dressed for the feast. "Hurry," I kept shouting! "He's on His way – our Bridegroom has already left and is on His way to pick us up!!!" There was much laughter and happiness as we all helped button up buttons, grab the other shoe for people, hand people belts for their trousers, we zipped up the backs of dresses, and did whatever was necessary to help "the family" get ready for our groom.

His arrival was so close that we began to run along on the housetops from roof to roof. We were "coming up higher" to be ready for Him. There was a sense of seriousness and great urgency about our work, for only those that were completely dressed and ready for the bridegroom when He arrived, would be allowed to stay at the Wedding Feast and enjoy the celebration. This celebration was the one to end all celebrations!

But what does this mean for Mom's and their children today?

ARE OUR FAMILIES READY?

Where the church once thought, "Jesus is coming soon," the trumpeter has now taken his place, and the call of God in the Spirit has begun to sound the alarm. The sleeping giant (the church and all those who are called) must awaken and be ready...for the bridegroom is at the door! Those that ignore the call, are in danger of being evicted from the Feast. (Matthew 22:1 – 14). Are you and your family ready?

There is a strong sense of urgency in the hour we live in, to fully embrace the call in the Spirit to train up our young men and women of God. Merely "being a good person" is not what I'm talking about. *The Mom Ministry* is about cultivating an atmosphere in our homes (and spheres of influence) that helps them seek after the things of the Spirit of God, be on fire with His presence, and sold out to Jesus.

There is a window of grace and opportunity that the Lord has given us to prepare our children for what's ahead. But the time is now. This urgency in the Spirit is like none the church has ever experienced before. It will cost us everything, but we will gain even more, the Spirit of Jesus Himself. He is prepared to meet us and consume us with His presence, grace, and wisdom in every step.

We can either embrace it and please our Father, or ignore it and miss out on the greatest blessing of our lives and answer for it later.

GOD HAS A MESSAGE FOR YOU

We live in a day and age that would blow our Great-Grandmother's minds! Yes, modern conveniences and technology have made child rearing much easier. We have a "time-saving" device for virtually every task on the market. Disposable diapers, disposable diaper bagging systems (for an odorless disposal), wet wipes, wet wipes warmers, `ready-made" and disposable bottling systems for their feeding, and this is just for starters.

By the time our kids reach Kindergarten, they are reading and operating complicated electronics such as computers, DVD players, and surfing the "net". Millions of dollars are spent each year, by young parents doing all they can to acquire the latest teaching programs for the computer, and the most up-to-date seminars for family development and child rearing. And as long as there are parents, we will continually be looking for the best way to give our children more than we had. And so it goes...from generation to generation. But, God has a message for this generation of mothers. It's for all who will listen and heed it. It's the key to unlock God's power and release it in your home, to prepare them and all those around you for Jesus' return.

To lay a good foundation for *The Mom Ministry*, I'd like to share Isaiah 61 with you. The day I began writing this book, the Holy Spirit led me to pray this passage of scripture. I continued to pray it daily as I wrote. The more I did, the more I saw that it is indeed God's purpose for each of us – and one of the messages He wants to impart through this book. The truths in Isaiah 61 are the essence of the purpose of "*The Mom Ministry*".

I urge you to not rush through these next few pages. If you're like me, when you've found a new book that you are very interested in reading, it's a temptation to buzz through because we're so eager to dive into the meat of the message. But there are truths that we must savor and digest slowly, so that the Spirit can plant it deeply in our hearts and lay them as foundation.

I believe God wants to do something mighty before we go any deeper into "*The Mom Ministry*". On the next few pages, I've included the written words to this powerful passage of scripture. I'm a firm believer that the Word of God is unchanging, living and active, and is for US – TODAY! As you open your heart and let it take root in your life, God will do things in you that you never dreamed possible.   There is power in His Word to change your life and circumstances.

As you read the passage, it's vital that you read it in a personal way. Read it as if you were saying it to yourself and family. Read and pray it out loud as many times as necessary until you believe it in your heart. God truly wants to perform His word in and through you every day. I encourage you to do this daily, and watch it not only grow down deep and take root, but also grow like a mighty tree of life in you. The fruit will be eternal and more satisfying than anything you've ever experienced before.

Isaiah 61

**The Spirit of the Sovereign Lord is upon me,
Because the Lord has anointed me to preach good
news to the poor. He has sent me to bind up the
brokenhearted, to proclaim freedom for the captives
and release for the prisoners,
To proclaim the year of the Lord's favor
and the day of vengeance of our God
To comfort all who mourn,
To provide for those who grieve in Zion –
To bestow on them
a crown of beauty instead of ashes,
The oil of gladness instead of mourning,
and a garment of praise
instead of a spirit of despair.
They will be called oaks of righteousness,**

a planting of the Lord for the display
of His splendor.
They will rebuild the ancient ruins and restore the
places long devastated;
They will renew the ruined cities
that have been devastated for generations.
Aliens will shepherd your flocks;
foreigners will work your fields and vineyards.
And you will be called priests of the Lord,
You will be named ministers of our God.
You will feed on the wealth of nations,
and in their riches you will boast.
Instead of their shame
my people will receive a double portion,
And instead of disgrace they will
rejoice in their inheritance;
And so they will inherit
a double portion in their land,
And everlasting joy will be theirs.

"For I, the Lord, love justice;
I hate robbery and iniquity.
In my faithfulness I will reward them and make an
everlasting covenant with them.
Their descendants will be known among the nations
and their offspring among the peoples.
All who see them will acknowledge that they are a
people the Lord has blessed."

I delight greatly in the Lord;
My soul rejoices in my God.
For He has clothed me with garments of salvation
And arrayed me in a robe of righteousness.
As a bridegroom adorns His head like a priest, and as a
bride adorns herself with her jewels.

For as the soil makes the sprout come up and a garden causes seeds to grow,
So the Sovereign Lord will make righteousness and praise spring up before all nations."

The truth is:

God wants to *establish* this powerful passage of scripture in your life, home, and the life of your children. It's His Word that has the power to change us. God wants to establish His word in the lives of your maternal children, paternal children, adopted and step children. He wants to perform it IN you and THROUGH you. Do you believe that today?

Let's look at what it means for God to "establish"[1] His word in us. The American Heritage Dictionary says, "establish" means,

"1. To make firm or secure.   2. To settle in a secure position or condition.   3. To cause to be recognized and accepted.   4. To found.   6. To introduce and put (a law, for example) into force.   7. To prove the validity or truth of."[ii]

God desires to secure you and your children in the truth of His word. He desires to write it on your heart and make it a living reality in your every day life. Knowing it's true isn't enough. But living it, and allowing God to "prove the validity of it's truth" in our home life, is truly a work of His spirit and is God's plan for our lives. It's the only path to achieving the REAL dreams that have been placed inside each one of us.

CHANGE IS COMING

The word of God is like a living seed that must be planted deeply in the good soil of our hearts. As we water it daily, by hearing it, re-reading it, and meditating on it, faith begins to grow and rise up within us. After a season, good fruit comes forth. But it's a process that takes time and continuously doing what pleases God, with the right heart. So be patient with yourself and the process

Remember, God's word is the absolute truth! Despite what your circumstances look like. Believe it! For you and for your family! This may help you make it more personal.

THINK OF IT LIKE THIS

Let's look at Isaiah 61 more personally and see it in light of our every day lives.

It is true that "The Spirit of the Sovereign Lord is upon me" to discern the reason for my baby's cry. When I've tried everything else: the pacifier, her favorite blanket or position, the bottle, and my options have run out, I must remember, the "Spirit of the Sovereign Lord is upon me."

I must remember that "I am anointed" to speak the truth in love to my children who are testing which ways are righteous or not. "He has sent me to bind up the brokenhearted child" who has been disappointed by his best friend for the 14th time.

God will give me a sure word that will mend his broken heart when his pet is tragically killed by a speeding car.

"He has sent me to release" my son or daughter who has been locked up in the prison of thinking that they are NOT as good as the most popular kid in their class, or when he or she didn't make the final cut in volleyball try outs.

He has anointed me, as their Mother and minister, to comfort them when they mourn the loss of a dear Grandma who suffered greatly before going "home".

I am anointed by Almighty God to bestow upon my daughter the crown of beauty instead of ashes after being violated or raped by her date.

God wants to give my son, "the oil of gladness instead of mourning, and a garment of praise instead of a spirit of despair", when he is tired of the 6 month re-cooperation process from a near fatal car accident.

We must believe that our family "will be called oaks of righteousness, and a planting of the Lord for the display of his splendor," when the neighbors are gossiping and criticizing us because our family chooses not to watch the same movies they watch.

Mom's who minister choose to remember and believe that "we will be called priests of the Lord, and named ministers of our God", when going through the fiery hot furnace of sanctification, burning out the things of the world in our lives.

"Instead of their shame
my people will receive a double portion,
and instead of disgrace they will rejoice in their
inheritance; and so they will inherit
a double portion in their land,
and everlasting joy will be theirs". Isaiah 61:7

This is a passage and declaration of the year of the Lord's divine favor in our lives!   It's for us, today!

The good news is that God is in the business of restoration by taking a family and making it into something more beautiful than imaginable. Moms who minister are a work in progress. Daily, God is molding us into Christ's image. He wants to cloth you and your family in His glory. Dare to fully believe His word for yourself and your family! When we do, something amazing begins to happen...

CHANGE YOUR TALK AND IT WILL CHANGE YOUR WALK

"...I am watching to see
that my word is fulfilled."
Jeremiah 1:12

God has committed Himself to watch over His word in your life to perform it. The angels of the Lord are dispatched to bring it to pass. Though you do not see or sense them, as you pray and declare His word over your lives, Holy angels are at work all around you and your children.

Take Isaiah 61 and type it out and place it on the refrigerator where you and your family can be reminded of it daily. As you pray it daily, it will begin to overflow like living water and wash through your home. It's time to discover and enjoy the fullness of God's word for your family. Be a believer that believes all of God's word and is completely obedient to it. As you do, you will see God do miraculous and wondrous things.   Things so wondrous, they are beyond your greatest imagination.

"Now to him who is able to do immeasurably more than all we ask or imagine, according to his power that is at work within us, to him be glory in the church in Christ Jesus throughout all generations, for ever and ever! Amen."
Ephesians 3:20, 21

three

Look For The Dove

ook for the dove, follow peace, and stay adjustable." During one particular time of earnestly seeking the Lord concerning our family, these were the powerful words He spoke to me. Since then, God has used them to remind us to keep our steps centered in His will, regardless of what it 'looks' like in the natural.

When God speaks something to us, it is so profoundly simple and deep that it sometimes takes years to peel away the many layers and depths of it's meaning. Each layer of understanding is revealed as we seek Him more, walk in obedience, and receive light and illumination from the Holy Spirit.

About the time I began writing this chapter, the Spirit of God began to speak to my heart once again through this phrase. Again and again, these words would rise up in my spirit. They are a vital part of *The Mom Ministry.*

I SEE A DOVE

My husband, Andy, and I were in prayer one night with a woman of God who had come to join us for coffee. As we prayed, this dear sister in Christ began to speak what the Lord was impressing upon her heart. She shared that while praying with us, she saw a huge dove over our home. This touched my heart greatly, as I remembered that I most often related the symbol of the dove in scripture to the Holy Spirit. "What a beautiful picture," I thought, "the Holy Spirit covers our home and family with His spirit."

It was shortly after that time, God began to call my attention to the dramatic changes in our own lives and in our children's walk with the Lord. Since we became completely open to the movement of the Holy Spirit in our lives, we had become tremendously strengthened and blessed with an amazing measure of grace. Our boys began to encounter more hunger for the Lord and spiritual awakening. Powerful things began to happen in and through our family.

Is it a coincidence? No! I believe these words were prophetically spoken as the Spirit gave utterance. We received them, believed them, and began to see the Lord do even more in our home. Something powerful was released into the spirit realm concerning our family. THUS – a CHANGE was initiated. It was something powerful that directly activated the further plan of God for our lives.

A few weeks later, I was visiting a friend of mine who pastor's one of the local churches in our area. We were discussing and praying about the mighty work of the Holy Spirit that is taking place in our region and nation. We came into agreement in prayer and worship together when the Holy Spirit moved on her heart to share this with me,

**"Lisa…I see a dove flying in the air, carrying a banner in its mouth. Yes, it is flying and flying…
and its you…you are the dove, Lisa.
I see you flying and carrying a banner.
I see you going and going, carrying this banner throughout the whole earth…"**

Was she saying I am the Holy Spirit? Not at all, please continue reading, so that I may share the interpretation with you. It is a most exciting thing for the Moms of this generation.

God was speaking, I could feel it in my heart. But it was in puzzle pieces. He was giving a little more of His revelation, a piece at a time. While she spoke, more of the puzzle pieces came together. That prophetic word was given to me on a Thursday morning. Two days later, a family from church dropped by to deliver some video games as a gift to our boys. When overwhelmed with excitement, my friend from church burst forth with, "Lisa, did you see the sky on Thursday?" "No," I replied, "I didn't".

"Well," she started, "it was more what my daughter saw. We were walking outside, and she grabbed my arm and said, 'Mom, look'! So I did", she said. "We looked up and in the sky we saw a huge cloud in the perfect shape of a DOVE – I mean it was a perfectly shaped dove." By this time, I was standing there completely awestruck! She had known nothing about the dove messages from the Lord. Later that day, my sister in law mentioned seeing the same thing as a confirmation. God indeed was saying something powerful through all of this.

Thoughts began to flood my mind, all having to do with doves. I remembered a few months earlier, just after a friend of ours finished writing his book, his wife came to sit next to me, during a tender moment in the spirit together. She handed me a gold and silver pin that was shaped like a dove. It sits on my desk where I write. She said that the Lord told her to give it to me. At the time, I had no clue what God was doing through this message of the dove. I only knew that it was bigger than I was (too big to fathom).

WHAT DOES IT ALL MEAN?

"What does this mean for me, " you're asking? "And what does this have to do with raising my children?"

As for the interpretation, I believe God is saying something prophetically to the Mom's of this generation. As we awaken in this move of God sweeping the globe and realize the urgency of the hour we live in, I believe that God is desiring to open our eyes to a final season of grace in the church. It's a season of great grace which beckons us to stand and move under the covering of the Holy Spirit (represented by the dove). The Holy Spirit is our mantle or covering (like the roof on our house). We must have His covering to be able to accomplish the great spiritual work of *The Mom Ministry*.

Doing so, releases the grace and power of God to do what ONLY He can do through us. God is calling this generation of Mom's to something far greater than simply raising healthy, polite, intelligent children who are trained to give all the right answers. There's something happening in the spirit that is requiring us to soar higher. It's God calling us higher, to raise up an army of young people who are equipped with power from on High, filled with revelation and light from the throne of God, and empowered to walk in miracles, signs, and wonders – like never before.

In the Book of Acts, Chapter 2, God's word declares that the Holy Spirit's outpouring will be upon *all flesh*...our sons and daughters too! It says that they will prophesy, dream dreams, have visions, and be filled with the Holy Spirit. God's word also promised that the latter rain (our day) will be greater than the former. God's word warns us in Acts 7:51 NOT TO RESIST the HOLY SPIRIT.

It's TIME, Moms! It's time for your children and mine. God is calling us higher to intercede for them, equip them and to impart in them all we have received from Him to accomplish all that they are called to do.

What's coming upon the land, including the battles in the Spirit, cannot be defeated with what *we* came into the battle with - it's an all together new season! That means we have a tremendous responsibility, like no other generation, to make sure we are pointing our children to intimacy with Christ, and doing whatever is necessary to help them understand the urgency of the hour.

It's time to be true believers that are sold out to Jesus, filled and empowered by the Holy Spirit. It's a call in the Spirit to every Mom today, whether a working mom, stay-at-home Mom, or full-time Ministry Mom, to LOOK FOR THE DOVE, FOLLOW PEACE, and STAY ADJUSTABLE.

It's the ministry and purpose of a lifetime. It's God's divine plan for our generation of mothers. It's beyond the four walls of the church. It's bigger than life – and God has chosen you and I to accomplish a specific part of His plan.

THERE'S MORE

"And when Jesus was baptized, He went up at once out of the water; and behold, the heavens were opened, and he (John) SAW the Spirit of God descending like a dove and alighting on Him".
Matthew 3:16 (AMP)

We must be IN THE SPIRIT to SEE IN THE SPIRIT. The call in the Spirit today, Moms, is to <u>make the time</u> to get in the Spirit, get in your prayer closet, cry out to God and don't STOP until you can LOOK and SEE the Spirit of God descending like a dove and alighting your children and household.

Alighting means:

1.   Burning; lighted. 2. illuminated; lit up. [iii]

Alighting means to shine and burn brightly, to come down and settle upon. The root form means also to relieve of a burden. We want our children to burn brightly with the light of heaven. With the light that dispels every form of darkness, that drives the forces of the enemy back in their schools, in our homes, neighborhoods, cities, and the nations. God wants to use them to make an eternal impact, wherever they go. He desires to relieve you of every burden. The Holy Spirit's purpose is to hover and cover, to empower us in this final hour. James 4:2 tells us that "you do not have, because you do not ask God."

In prayer today, ask the Holy Spirit to do for your family, what He did for Jesus. Ask Him to rest upon them, to relieve them of their burdens and to draw them close to Jesus. Ask Him to illuminate their lives so that they will shine and burn brightly with the light of Jesus.

And as you do so, pray confidently, believing that praying the word of God is one of the most powerful forms of prayer there is. A friend of mine calls it, "putting the Word on it," and that is exactly what it is. The Bible says the angels of the Lord hearken to His word. So as you pray God's word, put it on your children and believe in your heart that God will do it. He has no favorites. If He'll do it for one, He'll do it for you.

WANT IT. PRAY IT.
SEE IT HAPPEN.

The Mom Ministry is a work of the Holy Spirit. It's a call to seek God like never before for the destiny of our children to be brought forth into the natural. It's a call to come up higher. The war will indeed be won on our knees and in the spirit, as we use the full armor that

God has given us. This work cannot be done apart from abiding in Jesus intimately through prayer and the word. God's word declares that:

**"It's not by might, nor by power,
but by my spirit," says the Lord of hosts.
Zechariah 4:6 (KJV)**

THE BURDEN

It takes a sincere Mom who wants with all of her heart to see her children become all that God promised in His word that her children can be. This God-given desire brings forth a burden that compels us to pray fervently. If you seek Him, cry out to Him and pray in the Spirit – they shall be released to be all that God said. The plans of the enemy WILL be cut off from their lives.

Their lives will be turned around and become what God's word says, (but not apart from intercessory prayer). God's plans are accomplished through prayer, and walked out through a humble heart that believes. Take a moment and ask yourself the following two questions:

1) **"AM I DESPERATE for God"?**

2) **"AM I DESPERATE enough for my kid's to be on fire for God, that I seek Him daily"?**

THE DOVE MAKES ALL THE DIFFERENCE

With the eye of faith, John saw this, and it will take no less for us. God's word says that it's impossible to please God without faith. The dove symbolized peace (a virtue of grace) and harmony to a worshipper by God. In the Old Testament, dove wings were revered as love symbols.

Meditate on this truth with me for a moment, "Jesus did not begin his ministry until the dove (Holy Spirit) descended upon and entered him." Why was that? His Spirit upon us is required to do His work. When Jesus began His ministry, He began by quoting Isaiah 61 – announcing that the Holy Spirit's anointing was upon Him. And so it must be for us.

Why do we find ourselves frustrated and disappointed when we look at our children and see clearly they are not living a life that is sold out to God. We know that the Holy Spirit must be completely covering their lives and filling them in order for that to happen.

Pushing them to be Christ-like in their own strength is wrong and impossible. It will lead only to a yoke of heaviness, condemnation, frustration, strife, and bitterness. It takes the grace and presence of the Holy Spirit upon each of our lives to do all God is calling us to do.

We know from scripture, it begins with a real, authentic, relationship with God our Father, through Christ Jesus, first. And that's just the beginning. The Book of Acts speaks of something even more than salvation. Jesus told His disciples to go and wait for the gift of the Holy Spirit that would empower them to reach the world with His power and truth. It is out of that daily overflow that miracles, signs, and wonders are performed through us, also. The purpose is not so that we can mesmerize others with great power, but to cause unbelievers to believe in Jesus.

If we don't see this happening in our lives and homes, then, we have a responsibility in the ministry of being a Mom to pray it in! I am not implying that challenging ungodly behavior or disciplining our children is to be ignored or neglected. It's necessary and Godly to do so. But we must be careful to not do so WITHOUT seeking the Lord before and after. It will take the grace and anointing of the Holy Spirit every time to see their lives changed.

LIFT YOUR EYES
LOOK FOR THE DOVE

We don't have to become discouraged by what the present condition looks like! Look for the dove and continue praying, knowing that God rewards those who diligently seek Him. Many times in scripture those who were to be ministered to needed to "look up" before they received.

Position yourself to receive by lifting your eyes upward. Look for the dove today and be encouraged. Help is on the way to a praying, humble heart. The dove (Holy Spirit) will descend upon the lives of our children – as we pray that Jesus will make Himself real to their hearts and lives. As we pray and believe, the Holy Spirit can make it very hard for them to say "no" to Him. Remember Jonah?

Our prayers put pressure on the enemy. More than that, your prayers of humility and faith to the

Father, terrify him. That's why the devil works so hard to distract you from doing so. We must stand in the gap and exemplify a life that is under the same covering that Jesus had. A life that is radically obedient to God's direction and word. We must be living a life that is covered in His presence and is pouring out His grace, in order for them to see Christ in us.

The Holy Spirit is powerful, perfect, and real. As I wrote today, I heard the Spirit of the Lord say:

> *"Mom's...pray for the covering of My Holy Spirit upon your households. Like the dove that carried the olive branch in it's mouth to declare to Noah and his family that it was TIME to see life spring forth, so get ready to step out of the boat. As it was in the days of Noah, so it is for you - a new season. When you pray, boldly declare in the spirit that it is TIME for new life to spring forth in every life that is in your household. Declare it in the spirit, using the authority I have given you in the Name of Jesus. Declare that it is TIME for them to come out and step into the light of My grace and truth in their lives. Declare that IT'S TIME to be restored, revived, and refreshed, and that your household will serve the Lord, completely...and I will establish it for you, according to my word", says the Lord.*

THE DOVE

"Doves in the ancient world represented symbols of maternal nurturing where the mother who deeply loves her children is more than a caretaker. She rears them well and equips them for stability and prosperity in life. The Holy Spirit descending upon Christ in the form of a dove signified the Father's unending love for His Son who gave Himself so freely for the sins of mankind.

John the Baptist, recognizing the Holy Spirit in its dove form, unveiled the paternal and maternal union of God that brought Christ into the world and would soon birth His church. It was for this reason that John acknowledged Jesus as the Lamb of God who takes away the sin of the world. More than his confirmation of the appearance of the promised Messiah was involved. It also looked forward to the purpose and finished work of Christ's appearing. That was His body, the church, being born into the world. See John 2 for more study". [iv]

**"And the Holy Spirit descended upon Him
in bodily form like a dove, and a voice came from
heaven, saying, 'You are My Son, My Beloved!
In You I am well pleased and find delight!'" Luke 3:22**

The dove precedes the affirmation and approval of our Father. What a glorious day in our lives when we come to a place in God where we sense His blessing and delight over us. This in itself brings a deep change and inner work in the Spirit that causes everything in ones life to change.

The Mom Ministry is about being covered by and intimately related to the One True, Living God. He desires an intimate relationship with you 24 hours per day, 7 days per week. He desires a love affair with you, like you've never imagined before. It's about going beyond the doorway, past the kitchen, beyond the living room, and straight into the inner chamber with Him. Beyond the veil, where you are lost in His love and covering, He will consume you with His own heart and life changing presence. Out of this precious relationship with Him, your prayer life will be a fragrant offering to Him. And it will move His heart to move His hand on behalf of your family.

A FAITH OF THEIR OWN

When our children's Christianity is no longer because they've been raised in a Christian home, or because it pleases Mom and Dad, that's the moment that their Heavenly Father becomes real in their hearts and lives. This change happens the very moment our children hear His voice and respond for themselves. We must never give up on them. We must never stop loving or praying for them. God didn't give up on us, no matter how stubborn we were. Likewise, our prayers must never cease. We must never let our hope die out.

The fruit that comes from *The Mom Ministry* is eternal and due to the dove descending upon our lives. While walking the earth, though Jesus was literally God and man, He Himself did not begin His ministry without the Holy Spirit's covering upon Him. In this hour in history, it will take no less for us to successfully raise and minister to our children.

That's what it will take for them to live out their destiny and walk the genuine walk of a disciple. It's the only thing that will be able to protect us through the battles and trials ahead. To try and operate without it is simply "dead religion".

Today, by faith, you too can, "LOOK FOR THE DOVE, FOLLOW PEACE, and STAY ADJUSTABLE". Then, teach your children to do the same, and watch what God will do!

four

A Revelation From God to Mothers

**"...an oracle his mother taught him"...
Proverbs 31:1**

roverbs 31 is perhaps the most well known passage of scripture dedicated to women in the Bible. It's potent, and filled with practical ways of impacting our children and future generations. The opening verse makes a statement that sets the stage for this chapter, and for the message in *The Mom*

Ministry. Proverbs 31 is more than a picture of the ideal woman of God, scripture refers to this passage as an oracle taught by a mother.

She committed herself to raising a son who was God-fearing and who desired wisdom above all other things. The Spirit of God not only used this woman to impact a generation long ago, but it also speaks today, to a generation of Mothers who have the awesome task of raising the generation that may usher in the return of Christ.

Ask yourself the following question:

"If I knew that my children belonged to the final generation before Jesus' return, would I raise them differently"?

How does this message of long ago, impact our Motherhood today? How can our roles in motherhood serve the purpose of an actual ministry to and through our children?

In a time in history where careers, homebuilding, and satisfying our personal goals and dreams is the primary focus – this need to minister to our children rings loud and clear. God spoke clearly to my heart that **it's time to sound the alarm:**

God intends our "mothering" to be one of great eternal purpose and fruitfulness. God is desiring to birth a mighty move of the Spirit through our generation of Mothers. It's a generational move in the Spirit.

Like our Proverbs 31 Mom, we must hear the call and make a commitment to raise our children with an eternally minded viewpoint. It's time for each of us to evaluate what our primary focus really is. God's plan for us is like no other generation. Seeing our motherhood as a ministry is a gift to those who choose to embrace it. It's liberating and frees us from feeling defeated. By looking more deeply at Proverbs 31:1, we can see how. This chapter in scripture is referred to as "an oracle", which in today's language means: "a command or revelation from God". Let's take a look at it in greater detail.

EUREKA

The word "revelation" means, "opening the eyes to"; "to see through"; "recognize", "realize", "make certain of", "identify". Another great word to describe "revelation" – is "EUREKA".

If ever there was a time for women of God to step forward, it is now. It's time to make the decision to raise children who desire Godly wisdom and the things of God more than fame, power, fortune, and Nintendo! Our roles as ministers to our children needs to be recognized, identified, and embraced.

If there's a revelation that needs to be received today, it's that our children are truly in need of ministry by Mother's that are committed to minister to their mind, body, and spirit. Motherhood is more than meeting their needs physically, practically, and psychologically. It's about ministering the presence of God to them on a daily basis.

It's a ministry of faithfully interceding for them; blessing them (not cursing), teaching them, and helping them memorize the word of God. It's a ministry of exemplifying worship at home (not just at church on Sundays). It's confronting sin, and after prayer and direction from the Holy Spirit, re-directing them back to the heart of the Father.   It's living a life before their eyes, that is radical for loving, serving, following, worshipping, and passionately seeking God.

New Millennium Mom's must understand the magnitude of our role as mothers. Perhaps it was our Proverbs 31 Mom's own mother's words, that instilled in her the knowledge that within her was something of priceless value. God may have revealed this to her by the Holy Spirit or through a Spiritual Mother that God sent to cross her path. Perhaps the Lord revealed it to her through her own trials and quiet times of revelation in His presence. Perhaps she too had a moment that was an eye opening "EUREKA, " that she had only one life to live.   She had an incredible God-given opportunity to raise a child with a heart to lead in wisdom, and perhaps change the world. We too, may have such an opportunity, but we first, must embrace the privilege to minister to them.

What has God been whispering to your heart about your children or grandchildren and their future to make an eternal difference in the world?

~~~~~~~~~~~~~~~~~~~~~~~~~~~~

This would be a great time to pause, pray, and ask the Lord to show you His view of the destiny of your children. Ask Him to reveal His heart to you concerning them. Then, journal what He whispers to your heart, praying for them as you do.

~~~~~~~~~~~~~~~~~~~~~~~~~~~~

**"Like arrows in the hands of a warrior
are sons born in one's youth." Psalm 127:4**

I believe our Proverbs 31 Mom was a woman of vision, who saw her children as more than the fruit of her affections for her husband.   *The Mom Ministry* is one that comes from the heart of a mother who desires to see her children become all that God intends them to be.   She is willing to pay the price to see that happen.

A Mom who ministers, uses every bit of passion and persuasion within her heart to reach the heart and mind of her children with the truth of God's purpose for their life.   Viewing our role as a ministry is no longer an option.   We must first recognize, then use every teachable moment to plant the seeds of righteousness deeply into the soil of their hearts.

LOOK FOR GOD'S PURPOSE
LISTEN FOR GOD'S VOICE
IN EVERY CIRCUMSTANCE

Motherhood is more than just trying to make it through the day without another trip to the emergency room.   Though days like these are all too often a reality, we must pray that God keeps our eyes fixed on the eternal ~ and look for the opportunities to minister in the midst of every circumstance.   We must believe that the "steps of the righteous are ordered by the Lord," Psalm 37:23 (King James Version).   Believe that He allowed today's trials and struggles to reveal Himself to you in a new and deeper way. No matter what trial or persecution we are facing, we must remember and believe that God is always in control. He is bigger – and has a purpose for our present pain. No matter how bad it is, God is working all the things in your life together. He's working them out for good for those who love Him and are called according to His purpose.

We must see our children, and each day with them, through the eyes of faith and His word. We must look at it in two ways, both earthly (in preparation) and eternally (to rule and reign with Christ). Raising them with our sights fixed on eternity will keep our priorities in line, help minimize the magnitude of the trials we are currently facing, and help lift our eyes to our Hope which is Christ Jesus Himself.

Being a mother is not just about nurturing and caring for our young, it is the journey that God chooses to transform **us**. God uses our daily situations to transform us, by refining and molding us into the image of Jesus. Our children are the vessels He uses to test, try, and bless us.

TURNING POINTS

When was the last time you enjoyed REAL PEACE within your heart and through your Motherhood? Has it been a while since you've enjoyed yourself as a Mom? When was the last time you reveled in the enjoyment of being God's unconditionally loved daughter?

Has God been tugging at your heart that **there is more** for you as a Mom and for your children's future? Are you ready to ask the Lord to revolutionize the way you perceive your motherhood into a spirit-led ministry?

If so, simply pray this prayer with me and release every burden and frustration into His tender, nail-scarred hands. He's here and willing right now to give you something special in return.

Father,

I confess that I have not been letting your
Holy Spirit do the leading
as I raise _____.
(your child/children's names)
I confess that I need you to do it through me. Lord,
please teach me how
to get out of the way, and let you take over.
I ask you to take my role as a Mother, and make
me a minister of your
grace, wisdom, love, and truth, in our home ~
and even to the children you bring into my life that
do not have a mom who ministers to them.
Lord, make me a Spiritual Mother
to the emotionally and spiritually orphaned.
For the times I've failed and lost my way ~
I ask that the blood of Jesus wash over me.
I ask that you restore all that the enemy has
stolen from our family.
I ask for wisdom and the understanding to see the
hearts of my loved ones the way you do.
Lord, let my words and deeds
be an extension of You to them.
I ask this in the Name of Jesus. Amen.

Now, if you were sincere, believe that God heard your heart cry. Let His peace and grace fill your heart. You may be struggling with doubt and saying, "not me, you don't know me and all the mistakes I've made", or "it's just too late for me, my kids are already in their teens or are grown up and moved out". You may be feeling that you've failed too miserably – or perhaps your children aren't even speaking to you anymore. Has hopelessness set in because you believe it's too late?

The circumstances may look impossible, but I'm here to tell you that God is in the miracle working business of restoring the relationships that have been broken in your life. His specialty is taking an impossible relationship and transforming it, using one willing heart. He wants to use YOU. He'll take your situation and multiply it into a healthy life, home, family, city, and nation. To build up your faith in this area, read the story of Hosea and Gomer, in the Old Testament. Look at the heart of God's mercy and His power to change any family situation. Claim His word over your family each and every day and watch His spirit move mountains before you. God is ready and able to do a mighty thing in your family, starting today!

If you feel you need to, go back and say that prayer again. But this time, release any doubts and fears and embrace the truth that God is all-powerful and able to do above and beyond what you are asking Him to do.

AM I WILLING?

Think about the above question for a minute. Don't hurry in your response. Are you willing to let God be God? To take your motherhood and transform it into what HE wants it to be? Are you willing to lay down your OWN goals and ideas of what you believe it's all about? Are you willing to lay down the ambitions and dreams that YOU value to be the Mom that God has called you to be? If you can answer yes to these questions, then you are ready. You can expect God to do the miraculous in your home ~ starting today!

Are you willing to commit to teaching your child the very real purpose God has for his or her life? Are you willing to lay your motherhood down on the altar, and let your own efforts as a mother die so that God can resurrect HIS idea of motherhood through you?

The Mom Ministry is about surrender. Surrendering all we hope to accomplish, and all we desire to see taking place in and through our children. Only then can we can allow the Holy Spirit to jump in the driver seat and do the driving for us.

What I'm talking about here is not merely a positive-mental attitude to "Mother" our children with. It's a journey of faith and discovery for you and for your children. Ask yourself, "What IS God saying to us today? What IS He wanting to accomplish through me"? If this IS the final generation of Mothers that may walk the earth before Jesus returns, what would our mission be? How would your priorities change?

IT'S NOT ABOUT PERFECTION

It's almost a relief to read Proverbs 31 with the understanding that the almost "perfect portrait" of a wife and mother in that passage, was truly a mere human. If you're anything like I was while reading and studying it, you've thought to yourself, "how can I possibly live up to that level of expectation as a wife, and especially as a mother?" When I first began my journey with the Lord, it sounded more to me like, "The Proverbs 31 – "PERFECT Mother". And let me tell you, I did not feel motivated after reading it.   On the contrary, I felt rather defeated.   I saw it as an unattainable goal for someone like me.

But as I grew to trust Him more, the Lord began to unlock the meaning of how faith and His grace operate in my life. Today, I read the story with hope, as I remember that God took her broken beginnings and used her to bring forth and raise the King who rebuilt the glorious temple.   How did He do it? By God's grace and her willingness to obey.

In turn, God desires to use us to speak and pray His will, blessings, and purposes into our children's lives and future. It's a holy work… a ministry of His love, transforming power, and grace.

To see this happen in our lives, we must let go of all past failures and let the grace of God come in and transform us.   He'll bring mercy, forgiveness, and healing to every broken place that you give over to Him. Pray as you humbly obey what He gives you to do – and trust that His timing is perfect. He's faithful! He's faithful!

PROVERBS OF
THE MOM MINISTRY

The Mom Ministry is one of being a servant through sacrifice and obedience, but also one of great rewards. It's a journey of eternal destiny for both our children and ourselves, and is released through a heart set ablaze for Jesus!

As I studied Proverbs 31, I began to make a list of all the many powerful ways the Spirit of God moves through women of God. I'd like to share it with you today and ask you to place a check by the ones that you have sensed God displaying through you. During your prayer times, the list can be used to pray that they will be established in your life. Guard against discouragement as you read and find areas that the Lord is still changing in you. Instead, read and pray with an honest and thankful heart for all God has already done in you. Then, expect God to answer ~ believing wholeheartedly that it is His desire to see you walking in the fullness of His word. God's grace is poured out on every willing and humble heart.

- **She teaches her children the ways of God (verse 1-9)**
- **She is noble (verse 10)**
- **She is worth far more than rubies (verse 10)**
- **She brings her husband good, not harm – He has full confidence in her (verse 11 & 12)**
- **She works with eager hands (verse 13)**
- **She brings food from afar (verse 14)**
- **She rises early in the morning to provide food for her family and helpers (verse 15)**
- **She is keen in business and earns a profit (verse 16)**
- **She is strong for her tasks and works vigorously (verse 17)**

- She helps the poor and needy (vs. 20)
- She keeps her family clothed (verse 21)
- She selects fine fabrics and makes things beautiful (verse 22)
- She is productive and contributes to the household (verse 24)
- She is strong and dignified, not worried about the future (verse 25)
- She speaks with wisdom and faithful instruction (verse 26)
- She does not waste precious time (verse 27)
- Her children bless her, her husband praises her (verse 28)
- She is exceptional (verse 29)
- She fears the Lord (verse 30)
- She cares for herself
- She cares for her children
- She cares for her husband
- She cares for her community

There isn't a doubt in my mind that this is God's desire for our generation of Mothers. It's what God wants to do today, through you and I. It's for what's ahead. How comforting to know, God isn't looking for a perfect candidate, just a yielded, willing vessel that His spirit can flow through and transform. His grace does all the changing within, as we obey Him and yield to His process in becoming the woman of God He desires.

It's not about perfection, it's about "letting God be God" every moment of our lives, and trusting... that His plan works!

five

Son of My Vows

"O my son, O son of my womb,
O son of my vows..."
Proverbs 31:2

I n Proverbs 31:2, a Mother begins by addressing her child with a great expression of her emotion and love toward him. In this passage, she briefly, yet passionately expresses her acceptance of him. She is grateful to her heavenly Father for hearing her heart cries. She conveys to him God's own love for her, in that He has given her this child. She cherishes him, and makes it a point to verbalize it to him.

She emphasized that he was MORE than a boy. More than a son! He's more than the son of her womb, but the son of her vows. He is in fact, an answer to her prayers. Her words are truly an incredible example of *The Mom Ministry*. Her vocal expression and acknowledgement of God's manifested love in giving her this precious child, ministers to his spirit and blesses her own soul.

When was the last time you looked at your child and thought, "you are an answer to my prayers"? Are our lives as Mom's today, so busy or filled with 'things to do' that we don't express this truth to them? What a thought. What a warning for each of us to heed the times.

NO ORDINARY CHILD

How far do we go to make it a point to emphasize to our children, that they are not ordinary but are truly cherished. They are so much more to us than JUST our kids. We must express to them that they are more important than all we own, and all we accomplish in life. They are a gift from God to us! It's truth and they need to hear it. Do we express this to them?

Scripture tells us that while in our Mother's womb, we are known by God. Speaking forth the purposes and promises of God over their lives defeats the enemy. Reminding them often that God has a plan for their life and knew them even in the womb will instill in them a powerful sense of purpose and value. We see this practiced especially in the Old Testament, where the blessing from the Father was considered one of the most valued possessions. They struggled for it at times because of its monumental value.

YOU ARE THE ANSWER
TO MY PRAYERS

Prayer is the starting point of releasing the blessing of God upon our children.   Then, we must speak words of blessing over them, as often as possible. These are the basics that will build a healthy, Godly home.   Prayer, love, and the Word of God are the foundational building tools for our homes.

"Do not be anxious about anything, but in everything, by prayer and petition, with thanksgiving, present your requests to God. And the peace of God, which transcends all understanding, will guard your hearts and your mind in Christ Jesus."
Philippians 4:6-7

We minister to every human being out of who we are.   And we become who we really are by communing intimately with Him daily. Spending time in the presence of a Holy God changes us to be more like Him. He literally "rubs off on us".

What do you do if your prayer life is currently null? Pray. Ask the Lord to help you begin afresh today! Pray some more, and ask the Lord to change your heart to discipline yourself to be a prayer warrior. One of the simplest truths I've learned to live by is that if I'm lacking in any area of my life, then I must ASK God for it (even if it's as basic as needing a healthy prayer life). One of the best prayers to pray is, "Lord, teach me to pray." When you ask, remember that God's word says:

> **"... you do not have because you**
> **do not ask God".**
> **James 4:2**

> **"...ask and you will receive, and your joy**
> **will be complete."**
> **John 16:24**

> **"...apart from me you can do nothing."**
> **John 16:5**

It is in this time of prayer that we die out to our own desires and expectations of the day, and surrender to the Holy Spirit's guidance and perfect plan. Prayer is the lifeline, to our life-source, Jesus. Out of His own example, we saw the perfect model of a life completely surrendered to the Father. We are told in God's word that daily, even while it was dark, He arose to seek the heart of His Father. Each day, He surrendered all that He desired and took on the purpose of God for His life.

As we pray and seek Him, we cover all that is ahead for our day. God hears and downloads within us the appropriate balance of grace, truth, gentleness, goodness, and faith – that our day will demand. It is here that His life is released into our every day needs – including all that we need for our children.

TO BLESS OR CURSE

One of the greatest truths I've learned about *The Mom Ministry*, is the power in a blessing. I had to learn the difference between the two, before I could truly be freed to build up my home. The Bible says in the book of James:

"With the tongue we praise our Lord and Father, and with it we curse men, who have been made in God's likeness. Out of the same mouth come praise and cursing. My brothers, this should not be. Can both fresh water and salt water flow from the same spring?"
James 3:9-11

James speaks of this in the chapter that is subtitled, "Taming the Tongue". He goes on to say in verse 2, "we all stumble in many ways. If anyone is never at fault in what he says, he is a perfect man, able to keep his whole body in check." In verse 5 and 6 he adds, "Likewise the tongue is a small part of the body, but it makes great boasts. Consider what a great forest is set on fire by a small spark. The tongue is also a fire, a world of evil among the parts of the body..."

To "bless" means to invoke divine favor upon, to praise, to make happy, to bestow well being and prosperity upon.

To "curse" means to bring evil upon someone by using words; to damn.

I know what it feels like, in the heat of the moment, to lose my wits and pour out angry words that I've later regretted (more times than I care to remember).

Likewise, I've seen the impact that words of blessing and affirmation can make in a home. It can be the difference between excelling and failing, stepping out and shrinking back, joy and sorrow, freedom and bondage. Our words can either be used as building blocks, that will build up our home and children's lives, or they can be used as a destructive sledgehammer to undo months or even years of building. A woman walking in wisdom uses her words to build up her family.

Our words can make the difference between a child that flourishes and a child that is locked up in fear. Words can hurt, or words can heal. Words can condemn or words can bring hope and set someone free. Words spoken in sincerity and the Spirit can lead a soul to Jesus.

God wants to use our words and heart to raise a generation of kids who know the truth: that they are fearfully and wonderfully made. God had a plan for their life, long before the foundations of the world. His plan for them is to use them to make a difference in the world, and lead the lost to Jesus Christ.

The Bible says, **"the tongue of the wise brings healing."**
Proverbs 12:18

Too many kids today are being turned out of homes that are full of anger and frustration and being led down a path of fruitlessness. It's time to stand up and be about our Father's business - fully. We have an opportunity to raise our children to be fully armed with the invincible weapons of the Spirit.

CHOOSE TO BUILD

Our tongue is a powerful tool. Scripture refers to it as being full of life or death. It can be used to build up or tear down our loved ones. Choose to use it to encourage and build up your family with words of blessing. It is powerful! Every human being on the planet needs to know and hear that they are a blessing and valued. Many insecurities in adults today stem from hurtful or destructive words that they received as children.

Let's take the time to not only show our children they are an answer to our prayers, but TELL them with sincerity, often! Watch and see what God does in your own life, and theirs. Watch the atmosphere in your household change overnight, by speaking words of blessing, affirmation, love and encouragement, at every opportunity.

Don't wait for them to be all that you believe they should be before you give them words of blessing. By faith, take the initiative and bless them with five times as many words of affirmation as corrective ones. Why? Because words of correction are five times heavier than the words of affirmation! Are you correcting them more than building them up? Ask God to cleanse your tongue with the blood of Jesus, and anoint it to bring powerful words of blessing and affirmation that will catapult your family forward in God's plan for them.

The world is filled with enough condemnation and judgment. We must insure that our homes are a place of refuge for them to come home to. It must be the place they get filled up with unconditional love and acceptance.

WORDS FROM THE THRONE
FOR EACH CHILD

It is at the feet of Jesus that our hearts are humbled and made ready to respond to each question our children pose. It's there, in the presence of Jesus, that He will lay specific things and scriptures on our hearts that are custom tailored to each of our child's daily needs. A healthy prayer life and daily study of God's word is NOT an option for any Mom who ministers to the needs of her child. Prayer is what Oswald Chambers calls,

"A Holy Occupation."

A lack of it is most often, the reason for divided hearts and homes. A radical change in every home begins with one person getting "sold-out serious" about prayer. The power of God released through that one humble, believing heart is enough to cause a domino affect through that home, it's neighborhood and an entire city.

WE'RE GOING SOMEWHERE

Get a hold of this! Our daily struggles in Motherhood are part of the process God uses to test and prove what He has given us during that time. They are designed so that we will continually die to self, and allow Christ to rule and reign within.

It's the place where we humbly come before His throne and receive mercy and grace. Our daily life and experiences with our children, are the proving ground. How often do we unnecessarily see our daily challenges as attacks from the enemy? When in actuality, many of them are tests and trials which cause Godly character to grow and take shape within us.

If you've prayed to grow deeper roots in your faith, and suddenly find yourself in the midst of intense trials with your children, you may very well be experiencing the answer to your own prayers. Let me share one of our family experiences to show you how God works to mold us.

CREATE IN ME A CLEAN HEART, O GOD

I remember the time I was focusing on teaching my oldest son, Andrew, the importance of our actions and the consequences that result from them. He had gotten himself into trouble on the bus ride home from school. It left him with a difficult set of circumstances to face afterward. Needless to say, my husband and I also needed to walk through the consequences with him. We piled in our van and went over to visit the other child and his parents to apologize.

I found myself telling Andrew over and over through the whirlwind of emotion I was feeling, "do you realize the outcome could have been much more serious than what it is right now?" "Do you realize what we COULD be facing right now, if it weren't for the mercy of God?" "If you knew it was wrong, and the small voice of the Holy Spirit was saying, 'don't do it', why did you go ahead and do it?" "Do you think that was very responsible?"

By the grace of God, we got through the situation. He humbly apologized, played with the boy outside, and we ended up having a great visit with the child's Mom and Dad over a cup of coffee. But there's more to the story...

A few days later, and still troubled over the ordeal, I found myself blaming my husband for part of the incident. Ever played the "blame game" with your spouse? "After all," I added, "you let him get away with so much more than I do", "I mean, you need to be a little more conscious of his behavior..."

Sound familiar? Ever felt a little self-righteous towards your spouse before? God help us...don't you know, the Lord listens to EACH and every word we speak? If you've walked with the Lord any longer than a month, then you too, know by now, that God has a quiet, but profound way of opening our eyes when we're blinded by our own self-righteousness and pride, doesn't He? I was in for a well deserved lesson in humility, as God continued working all around us to do something beautiful.

ATTITUDE CHECK

Less than a few days had gone by, when here came my loving correction – nestled inside a shiny white police car. I had taken a small paper route to collect extra income. It was just before summer began. It wasn't my choice of careers, but it worked well with my schedule so that I could be home during the day for the kids. I arose at 2:30 each morning and remember having approximately 40 stops to make. My goal each day was, "do the best you can, as fast as you can, *and get it over with*".

I distinctly remember one morning only having 4 or 5 more stops. I was driving, from stop to stop, zooming in and out, trying to save more time. Ever felt a little too safe? I mean, it's 4 am, for crying out loud. And what on earth would a police car be doing parked on the side of the road in the dark (on a side street). And what were the odds of a squad car being camped out in the middle of a nice subdivision, in the middle of the night? If he was lucky he'd only see one car every 30 minutes or so...until ME.

You got it, he got me as I rolled through the stop sign! I felt the physical sensation of panic hit my mind before I was able to pull over to the side of the road.

Here I was, thinking, "This can't be happening! Oh God, please, I ask for mercy, I think I forgot my license at home!" Pure panic gripped my heart as I prayed and scraped and clawed to find my wallet. "It's here somewhere, isn't it"? "I thought I grabbed it..." as I scurried around, checking my mirrors (watching for him to walk up). "This CAN'T be happening. Oh-h-h-h-h. I only had 4 – 5 more stops to go. Maybe he'll let me go. Oh, God, please..."

NOPE. I believe I got a dose of the same serum I dished out just a few days earlier." Not only had I self-righteously blamed my husband for the stress, I had forgotten how easy it is for a young boy to disobey the rules, and obviously, I had forgotten how easy it is for his mother too, also.

Instantly I got a fresh dose of understanding in a way I truly didn't want. Even so, God was at work in another way that was precious! So what does this have to do with my Mom Ministry? Let me explain.

After this ordeal with Andrew on the bus, he had been sent to his room (to think about it). But apparently, he decided to spend some time in prayer. He was searching for forgiveness from the Lord as well as peace for his thirsting soul. I had left him alone in his room for quite some time. I returned after he had thought things through a while. I looked over on his bed, and saw his bible laying open. I asked him how he was feeling and what he had learned from the whole experience, and he answered with something absolutely amazing and precious.

With a certain sense of quiet confidence, he looked me straight in the eyes and said, "while you were gone, Mom, I spent some time in prayer and then God led me to a verse, it's I John 1:9. It says:

"If we confess our sins, he is faithful and just
and will forgive us our sins and purify us from
all unrighteousness."
I John 1:9

"After I read this verse, Mom," Andrew said, "it was like God put something in my heart that made me *know* that whether or not the boy and his family forgive me for doing something wrong or not, JESUS has already done it. I know that I will be ok, I am forgiven."

There I was, standing in awe. WOW! This boy truly heard from God. Even more, the Lord had revealed to Him the secret of God's redeeming grace. It made all the pain and frustration worth it.

As I looked on, I noticed his boyish countenance was free and full of peace. I saw something in him that was beyond the boundaries of age and intellect. I saw right through to the peace in his soul. It left me in humble awe to see that my son, the son of my womb, the son of my vows, was led by the Spirit of God to seek Him in the midst of a trial. Knowing he had done so, without my prodding, left me completely thankful and humbled before God for His touch and grace upon his life.

I found myself in prayer shortly after, "Thanks, Lord. This has been an answer to my prayers and heart cries for my children." I was thankful for the lesson of humility as well. "Though it was so difficult to walk through these past few days, I see your mighty hand in it – working it all together for our good and your glory."

He hears us, and is faithful to answer us, when we call to Him.

IT'S NEVER TOO LATE

If you're children are already grown and your relationship is in desperate need of help, don't despair. Ask God to open a door for conversation, sit down with them, and have a heart to heart talk. It's NEVER too late to begin. The TRUTH is powerful and is unchanging. It is able to set every heart free that will receive. With prayer, and sensitivity to God's timing, God will give you the words that bring healing for mistakes in the past.

Let us embrace the ministry of being a blessing to them by teaching them that they are an answer to our prayers. What a gift! What a treasure they are – we feel God's love through them. From the warmth and joy that flood our heart with each new step they take, to the comfort we feel, when tears run down our cheeks and they come with a genuine hug to say, "it's going to be ok, Mom".

I recall a sad birthday I had one year – and God used my oldest son Andrew to speak His truth and love to my heart. It ended up turning my whole day around, as God used my little boy to minister to ME. As you read, you may recall some of your own tender memories.

We had just been called by a local car dealership to tell us that our credit didn't go through for some reason. So, they were asking that we return the beautiful new conversion van that we had purchased

14 days earlier. When we had left the dealership, they assured us that all was well, and we were happily handed the keys to this van that we had waited for such a long time to own. We had prayed and waited, felt peace about it, and didn't have any problems with our credit history until, 14 days later, they claimed we were denied the loan. After all these years, I still don't quite understand how it happened, but what we gained spiritually made it all worth it to me.

You see, I had just finished speaking with the salesman who gave me the sad news. As I hung up the phone tears began to stream down my cheeks. Disappointment had set in quickly. It was my birthday and this made it feel even worse. This van had been such a blessing to us, and I couldn't understand how this could have happened. None of it made sense – our credit was good, we had peace when we bought it, but somehow there was a mix up.

There I was, sitting in the living room, confused by the situation, disappointed, and full of sadness. I had gone to the "Word" and found myself searching for answers and some sort of consolation, when my oldest boy, Andrew, walked in the room (he was about 5 or 6 years old at the time).

"What's wrong, Mom," he asked in his little, tender voice? "Mom," he said, placing his small hand on my shoulder. "It's your birthday, God loves you and doesn't want you to be sad on your birthday, He'll make everything ok...". With those words, came the most beautiful sense of peace, as light broke through to my heart. They could have only been inspired by God – for truly GOD IS LOVE. In that moment, I felt it stronger than ever. His love pierced my broken heart. What happened between Andrew and I was from spirit to spirit. Enough to dry my tears and give me hope, that God was in control and the most important things in life, I already possessed. What more could I possibly need.

In that moment I was once again utterly humbled and thankful for the gift that I have in my son. That terribly disappointing moment turned to happiness and joy, in the blink of an eye. God used the precious heart of his little one to bring me the gift of peace. God uses our children to bless and minister to us. Oh, that we would have eyes to see and ears to hear every day.

That day, I saw Andrew in a different light. Not only as my beautiful son, but also as my brother in Christ.

How often are they God's messengers of hope and strength to us and carriers of the answers to our prayers? How often does God use them to remind us of the truly important things in life: the simple things, the lasting things (too many times to count). It's so easy for us to get lost in the countless responsibilities we carry as parents. The bills, making lunches, remembering to make the doctor's appointments, even keeping food on the table. This can go on and on, and without even realizing, it can lead to the very attitude that they are merely another responsibility (rather than what they TRULY ARE - a GIFT from God). They are the sons and daughters "of our vows".

In a world filled with distractions, truly important things and cares of life can distract us from the most essential needs we have – the recognition that LIFE itself is a gift from God. TIME together is a gift from God. LOVE between two hearts is a gift from God.

Are you feeling overwhelmed these days by the "craziness" of all that is scheduled? Are you feeling lost in the "To-Do" lists, the every day hustle and bustle? Struggling to find the time for what's truly most important?

The best remedy is to STOP. Just STOP for 60 seconds each day, take your child by the hand and walk outside for a "sit on the porch". Get down on their level, physically, and look them in the eyes. Hold their face with your hands and tenderly tell them:

- "your love is worth more than gold to me"
- "your simple love for fun and laughter – makes my heart happy"
- "you remind me that all that I think is important, is not as important as I thought"
- "you are an incredible kid – I'm so blessed to have you in my life"
- "how are you? I missed you today!"
- "I not only love you, I like you"
- "what can I do to be a better Mom to you?"
- "you're better than my favorite ice cream"
- "You make being a parent the best part of my life"
- "you are an answer to my prayers"
- "Know what I like best about you...?"
- "Have I thanked you lately for ..."
- "Did I ever tell you how we picked out your name?"
- "I see amazing things in you..."

Let's seal it in prayer...

Father God,

I pray you will give us a revelation of the riches in this
truth you've shown us in Proverbs 31.
Burn it in our hearts and minds, Lord.
Our kids are not merely our sons and daughters,
but are answers to our prayers – each and every day.
They are truly GIFTS to us from you - containers of RICH
and PRICELESS love, purpose, and destiny...eternally.
Use them to continue to impact our lives
and even in the world.
Give us eyes to see the way you do, Lord.
Thank you for them, Father.
Thank you for entrusting us with them.
As we journey toward our eternal home together, help
us MAKE the time to express to them, the beauty and
importance of their very lives.   Help us establish proper
priorities, where they are given the place of value they
are so deserving of.
In Jesus Name we pray, Amen.

six

What Time Is It?

he Tribe of Issachar (David's mighty men), knew the times (or seasons) and knew what they should do. This required wisdom that came from walking closely with the Lord. It's true that time is a big commodity, these days. We live in a world where time management seminars and books are almost a "must" to learn how to function in the business

world. God is calling the Mom's of the New Millennium to "come up higher" in prayer and worship. God desires to draw us into a greater level of intimacy with Him. This will bring greater levels of wisdom and understanding.

ITS ABOUT ETERNITY

One day, the Bible says, we will stand before the Lord and give an account for our lives. That is a very sobering thought. I believe we will see at that moment what an incredible gift time has been to us. As His children, God is expecting us to be faithful stewards of it and to bring Him glory with it. We were bought and paid for with a price. Each day we walk with Him, we need to lay the minutes of our day before Him and ask Him to direct each one according to His perfect plan.

I know a woman of God, who began her day on her knees with a pad of paper and pen. After spending precious time praising and worshipping God for who He is, she would inquire of Him and ask, what things He wanted her to do throughout her day. She would record each item as the Lord would give it to her. This was her daily assignment, to complete each task that the Lord had given her. At the end of her day, she knew, that all had been accomplished through His loving grace. Therefore, each day was a complete success. There was no room for regret, no room for imbalance, only peace and the fruit of a life that is supernaturally led.

We try so often to make our own lists and complete what everyone else gives us to accomplish except the most important one of all, the list that God,

Our Father has for us. Our future cannot change until we change what we are doing today.

There are seasons in our life, that seem to be so filled with responsibility, that we don't know how to juggle it all. In the midst of it all, it's so easy to forget that God has a divine plan for each day.

SPIRIT-LED SCHEDULING

Seasons such as an unexpected illness in your family, or the loss of employment (which forces you to take on two new jobs in its place), or an increase in rent, all can throw our schedules into a whirlwind. It can feel like it's pulling your family apart. Still, as believers, we must ask the Holy Spirit to point out areas of our lives that need adjustment and realignment. As you follow His leading and adjust the areas that He impresses upon your heart, He will keep all your affairs in order – and you'll see much fruit coming forth. The key here is to regularly evaluate your schedule, stay sensitive to whether or not things are in balance, and be willing to make the needed adjustments.

I made it sound so easy, didn't I? Yet, you and I both know it always sounds easier than it is. There are times that difficult adjustments need to be made (especially if we've been running on overdrive for a long period of time).

It's important to trust the leading of the Holy Spirit in each step. As you pray, obey and stay encouraged by the word, you will find yourself walking in sync with the Holy Spirit and see Him begin to do MORE through you, than you could have done through your own planning.

Before making any drastic adjustments to your life, that would require a major move or career change, it's important to seek out and follow sound, biblical counsel. Speak with your pastor, or a seasoned leader who is a spirit-filled man or woman of God. Look for confirmation and make sure God's will, way, and timing all line up beforehand.

Remember, the enemy "pushes us," but the Lord gently leads us (like a Shepherd).

"By wisdom a house is built and through understanding it is established;" Proverbs 24:3

I have found that God is faithful to confirm his direction to us, as many times as we need. God wants us to know in our hearts that it is truly His direction for us. He is not a God that would lead us into confusion. We have made the mistake too many times of running ahead without waiting for the confirmation and peace that comes when it's truly the Lord leading. And we've paid the price for it, too.

"Look for the dove, follow peace, and stay adjustable", are the words God spoke to our family to help us stay balanced. They remind us that God's will, God's way, and God's timing go hand in hand.

Obeying every directive from the Holy Spirit to re-align your life and schedule will require faith. You may look at the direction God is giving you and find fearful thoughts arising in your mind. Thoughts may come that tell you it's impossible to do what God is directing you to. Or, the enemy may work to cause you to doubt that it's truly God's leading in your life. He will lie to you at every turn and do all he can to discourage you from following the confirmed direction of the Lord for your family. He knows that imbalance is a snare, and will do all he can to keep you trapped on the treadmill of "busyness".

Fight it! Fight it with every ounce of spiritual strength you have in you – go against the flow if you have to. Make a declaration today, that the only thing that will rule and dictate the hours in your day, from now on, is God's plan for your life. Choose to live the Spirit-led life on purpose! This is impossible to do without God. But Luke 1:37 says, "With God all things are possible". Then get ready to reap a bountiful harvest of peace like a flowing river in your home, ministry, and career.

**"Know also that wisdom is sweet to your soul;
if you find it, there is a future hope for you,
and your hope will not be cut off."
Proverbs 24:14**

GOT A DAY PLANNER?
GOT A PALM PILOT?

"Busyness". It's the way of the world in many societies today. If we're not careful, it can starve our family from the time and attention they so desperately need! And it is deadly when we allow it to rob us of intimate time with the Lord.

Do you find yourself pushing it off and saying to yourself, 'I'll do it later', only to find, you are laying in bed with a list of undone duties racing through your mind? Are you writing notes to yourself, to remember to sit down with little "Bobby" and ask him how his day was? Or are you so overloaded that you're now writing notes to remind yourself to read the reminder notes? Listen, I've been there, and it's not fun!

There's no better time than the present to bring words of encouragement to one another.

I'd like to share a special moment that we had with my own Mom just before she "went home to heaven". She went home to be with the Lord just 6 days after 9-11. Mom was an intercessor who lived a lifestyle of prayer. And though it's always difficult to let go of one of your parents, because she knew Jesus, it was also a most glorious time with her spiritually. To live a life that is consumed with love for Jesus – is the best inheritance we can leave our children. The hope of heaven comforts their aching hearts when it's time for us to go home.

One of the most recent and profound memories we have with her took place 2 weeks before she died. It was the last time that my husband, Andy, saw her before she went "home". In fact, as he turned back to see her one last time before walking out the hospital room door, these were her last words to him:

"Andy, make sure you spend TIME with the boys.
Spend as much TIME with them, as possible…
They are so blessed to have a father in the home.
My children didn't have that growing up…
and it's so important", she said.

Although we didn't realize at the time, those would be her last words to him. There was a sense of urgency in her voice as she spoke. Looking back, the fact that they were the last words he would hear her say, makes it all the more meaningful.

What a tremendous call to keep our priorities straight. As she faced eternity and reflected upon the most important things in her earthly walk here – she felt urged in her spirit to impress us with the value and gift of TIME. I am coming to learn, it is perhaps one of the most important things she ever instilled in us, as parents.

The skill and grace of "balancing" our lives is another "book" topic all in itself. And it is my belief that TIME and BALANCE go hand in hand. It's a fruit of living a life completely devoted to God. But the TIME to express our love and appreciation will NEVER be there, unless we MAKE it a priority.

ON WHAT ARE YOU SPENDING MOST OF YOUR TIME?

Do you realize the things you give most of your time to are what you consider to be the most important in your life? Yes, we need to make a living, to put food on the table, to provide for our families, but how much of it gets carved out for the most important people God has given us? Are God and our kids getting their fair share? Or are they constantly pushed off, as if they are not as important as the other things in our "to-do" pile? Ask yourself today, and be honest.

If you find yourself struggling in this area, are you really serious about change? Then ask a good friend who knows you well, to give you a straight answer concerning your priorities of time with your children. Be prepared to accept it with a humble, open heart, then commit yourself to take it to God in prayer. There, you can receive His grace and love and follow up by asking Him to help you in every area of your weakness. He will help you change. And your entire future and family will be blessed for it.

IT'S TAKES TIME TO BRING HEALING

"...but the tongue of the wise brings healing."
Proverbs 12:18

Producing the fruit of tenderness, security, unity in the family, and value within our children will help keep them from veering off the road. If we don't take the time to express to our children how much we value them, the devil will be certain he puts someone in their path that will. And he will use it to lead them astray. Don't take this lightly! And don't think for a moment, it can't happen to you.

"Be self-controlled and alert.
Your enemy the devil prowls around like a roaring
lion looking for someone to devour.
Resist him, standing firm in the faith,
because you know that your brothers
throughout the world are
undergoing the same kind of sufferings."
I Peter 5:8, 9

Our kids not only need our love and hugs, they need to hear it, too! Fill them up with spirit-filled words of affirmation and solid beliefs that they ARE somebody of royal importance - to you and to God. We must be alert and act as their best cheer leaders and fan club – or the wrong influences will be. It truly boils down to a choice we make every day!!!

**"She speaks with wisdom,
and faithful instruction is on her tongue.
She watches over the affairs of her household and
does not eat the bread of idleness.
Her children arise and call her blessed;
Her husband also, and he praises her."
Proverbs 31:26-28**

One of the fruits we bear as we allow God to change us, is that our children will arise and call us blessed. Our husbands will also. But it starts with us. By asking God for wisdom and applying His word to our life, a transformation takes place within us that effects every area of our lives. Yes, it takes time, but good fruit that leads to joy, purity, and righteousness in our homes will spring up in due season. God is faithful to bless the acts of the righteous!

SPIRITUAL MOTHERING

This role thrills me each time I think of it. Part of our roles in *The Mom Ministry* is the privilege of leading our children to Christ, or at least, playing a major role in preparing them for it. This role is not merely for the ministers in our local church. There is a huge blessing in store for every Mom that dares to take the plunge.

At age 5, I led Andrew to the Lord in the back seat of our Honda on our way to Grandma's house. It was so precious! At age 3, we led AJ in the prayer of salvation on our back patio. Yes, God intended Mothers and Fathers to play the largest role in our children's spiritual development and growth. And

Mom, because of the tremendous amount of time you spend with them, you are most likely the one who will influence them most to be passionate towards the things of God.

Mom's are most likely to give our children the first lessons of learning about our faith in Christ Jesus. We can't leave it to our church to do. The task is far too big for Sunday mornings alone.

Today, God is calling us to be our children's Mother in the Spirit. This ministry is the most important privilege we are given. To train them to minister the presence of God through prayer, intercession, laying hands on the sick for healing, prayer for the captives to be set free, to help prepare them to teach and preach the gospel. All of these are part of *The Mom Ministry.* Whether our children are called to work in the marketplace, government or God's house, each and every one of us is called to be ministers of reconciliation. Being salt and light in the dark world and doing our part to release the Holy Spirit through our lives to restore and win the lost to Christ, is our mission.

In the Old Testament, Hannah is a beautiful example of this. She conceived, gave birth to, and prepared Samuel for the work of the Kingdom of God. Setting apart her own life and his, she dedicated him completely to God's perfect plan and Lordship. Hannah's heart was completely surrendered to God's will and the desire to bring Him the greatest possible glory.

God saw this and honored her prayer and pure desire by entrusting her with Samuel and blessing her with many more children. God in turn raised him up and used him as a judge-prophet that ruled Israel after the death of Eli. He served as a spirit-led magistrate, ruler, and governor. Samuel later trained up many to serve the Lord, and anointed King David as the King of Israel. The fruit of her sacrifice is eternal. It effected countless people, including you and I, today.

Imagine what our world would look like 20 years from now, if every believing Mom did the same with their children. What if each one of us took our ministry to our children THAT seriously? Heaven would be a lot fuller.

Take a few moments to journal
your thoughts and prayers concerning
God's plan for the Time He has
Entrusted you with.

Be open...

Wait and listen...

Then, do whatever He says...

seven

Dressing Them In Royalty

YOU ARE OF ROYAL DESCENT

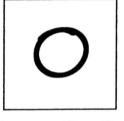 ne of the most valuable and beautiful truths we can instill in our children about our walk with Christ is our personal heritage in Christ as part of His royal family. We are truly the children of the Most High God. Our Master is the King of Kings and Lord of Lords Himself!

Through the blood of Jesus, atonement was made for our sin. We are washed and bought with His priceless and powerful love. It's the acceptance of this unconditional love that transforms our hearts and brings real change in our lives. In I Peter 2:9, we are told:

"⁹But you are a chosen people, a royal priesthood, a holy nation that you may declare the praises of him who called you out of darkness into his wonderful light. ¹⁰Once you were not a people, but now you are the people of God; once you had not received mercy, but now you have received mercy."

We were once nobody, but NOW we are the people of God and covered in His mercy. Now THAT'S somebody. It's as good as it gets! The mercy He lavishes on us changes our lives and attitudes and leads us to endless joy.

As we teach and exemplify for our children that, by faith, they are literally of "Royal" decent, we will be simultaneously sowing in them the true value that God places upon their lives. The truth of who they are in Christ will set them free.

As we value them in word and deed, it becomes possible for them to believe that God values them. What a void it fills in each of our lives, to know that we truly are something precious and irreplaceable. The truth that the God of all creation calls us His own, His royal priests, must be instilled in the heart of our children, in order for them to take God's vision for their life and run with it.

PRECIOUS, JUST AS YOU ARE

Who would argue that we live in a world where most are trying to "keep up with the Jones's", including our kids. It's a trap, filled with endless striving. The truth that they are somebody special if they have Christ, regardless of what they own materially, is emotionally and spiritually liberating.

It doesn't matter what you look like or who thinks you're great, what matters is what God thinks! Instilling this truth in our children is obviously God's idea of an award winning parenting skill!

While the Lord was leading Samuel, the Prophet-Priest, to the one to be anointed to be King of Israel, the Lord had a powerful word of wisdom for Samuel. Samuel thought that Eliab, David's oldest brother was the obvious choice. But God saw differently and taught Samuel a most valuable truth. When it comes to royalty and being chosen – God doesn't see things the way we do:

"But the Lord said to Samuel, 'Do not consider his appearance or his height, for I have rejected him. The Lord does not look at the things man looks at. Man looks at the outward appearance, but the Lord looks at the heart."
I Samuel 16:7

The truth is, every human being that knows Jesus Christ as Lord and Savior, is in God's eyes, of royal decent. The cream of the crop! Why? Because He is looking at the heart. The Bible says, those that have pure hearts, are blessed and shall see God, regardless of what the world says is acceptable and successful.

How do you see yourself? Do you see yourself as God does, as royalty? Royalty is something of an entirely different order. Royalty is about our bloodline. It's not based on whether we have earned it or not – but freeing us to be accepted and loved completely as we are. We see that in the lives of the royal family of England. In awe and amazement, the world looked on, each time Princess Diana took part in the most mundane daily activities. Why? Some of the reason was the wonder of her royalty.

The same truth applies to each of the sons of God. The Bible says we are God's royal priesthood. We have been set apart and cleansed, because of the blood of Jesus, who is the King of Kings Himself. Being a part of a royal family is special and can also be difficult. Not just anyone can be considered "royalty". Only those who qualify, or are "born into" the family, obtain the privileges and benefits of royalty. The benefits come through inheritance, not by works.

God is desiring that we instill this in our children. Being a member of God's family is truly being a part of a ROYAL priesthood (of the highest order).

"KING'S KIDS"

Here's a simple and fun illustration for you and your children. If you really want to make a lasting impression and help them grasp the fact that they truly are ROYAL in the spirit, here is an illustration you can use with your young ones and do together as a family. This could be done with a Sunday School Class, with some friends from the neighborhood, or at home with your family. It will make a lasting impression and instill in them a powerful bible truth.

For younger children:

1) Make, borrow, or purchase a crown or plastic tiara.

2) Help your child make a scepter out of rolled construction paper using glitter, glue, and plastic gems. For more fun, give them some costume jewelry to wear around their neck, and clip a towel or piece of fabric around their shoulders as their royal robe.

3) Give them the first choice in many of the day's activities.

4) If possible, celebrate by setting the table for dinner using candles and serve their milk or juice in a tall plastic goblet or cup. (Just like a real King or Queen might do).

5) At the dinner table, start with reading, then discussing I Peter 2:9, 10. Throughout the day, keep reminding them how blessed and good it is to be in the Kingdom of God.

6) Close the day, by praying together, using this passage of scripture. Thank the Lord for Jesus' shed blood that makes those of us who believe, a part of His royal family. Ask Him to help you live as a 'Kingdom-Kid' and make choices that show the world we are in Christ Jesus' family.

For older children:

1) Do away with the props used for younger children (unless you are feeling extra young at heart)!

2) At the dinner table: begin by asking the following questions to open a family discussion. Keep it fun.

   • "If you were a Prince or Princess, what would be your favorite thing to do?"

   • "What would be the hardest part about being royal?"

3) Emphasize the importance of using wisdom in making right choices as a Prince or Princess. For their decisions will affect the entire Kingdom (their family, their community, school, even our nation and world). Making right choices will help those who are not a part of the royal family, come alongside to be adopted in. It will help keep order, peace, and unity flowing.

4) Plant seeds of faith-filled ideas that God wants to give them the kind of life that will be used to bring His light to the nations of the world.

5) Ask one of them to read I Peter 2:9 - 10 out loud. Encourage them to look at the beautiful parallel within our Christian lives. By faith in the precious, royal blood of Jesus, we are grafted into God's mighty kingdom. Our decisions,

from that moment on, affect everyone in the Kingdom of God and beyond. Our lives, and Godly choices, reflect Jesus to outsiders of the Kingdom.   In the same way our ungodly choices turn people away from the Kingdom of God.

Seal it by reminding your children daily:

"God has an awesome plan for you!
You are chosen by Almighty God for greatness!
With Jesus as our King, we are filled
with His royalty and life!"

Loving Father,

I pray that you will give
me the grace I need to help my children
see and know deep within their hearts,
that the royal blood of Jesus
paid for their own heavenly royalty, in full.

Father, I pray that their spirit will catch
what you are saying to them through this teaching.
I pray that deep in their hearts,
they will sense how special and loved they are,
and how important it is to "shine" for Jesus,
that the world may know you and your love for them.
I pray also, Father, that they will be compelled to
cherish all those around them in the same way.
Thank You for drawing us deeper into your heart, Lord.
I Love You and Thank You.
In Jesus Name, I pray. Amen.

eight

The Power To Change

THE STRUGGLE

I t is still hard for me to watch old family videos (from back in the days when my oldest was a baby). Though I loved the film clips of Andrew's adorable smile and first steps, in the background of most of the footage, sits a young woman in our family who truly needed help. From where I am today, I can watch the videos and see the pain behind her all "made-up" eyes, and long curls, nice clothes, and laughter. In every scene she chews her gum nervously, rocks in the rocking chair in what appears to be a desperate effort to relax, and always seems to be looking for another cigarette. You can see she did everything with excellence, striving to be the best she could be in everything she did. Still, she was always edgy about the slightest thing, and never seemed satisfied with anything. Because of this, I remember her completely belittling her husband. She was always fearful that someone was going to think badly of her and him, and therefore, did all she could to perform well. It was as if she wasn't able to trust anyone.

I never saw anyone more terrified of being a mother. Fear was her way of life. Everything had to be just perfect for her children and family. If not, she was frantic. Her insatiable desire to plan everything stemmed from her fear that everything would not go perfectly. There never seemed to be any rest for her or for those she lived with.

Running to and fro, she searched for the best schools – so that when her children were ready to enter Kindergarten, it was already mapped out. She was always afraid everything wouldn't get done, or that things were going to fall apart. Her race always seemed to be against the clock. This explained her restless sleep every night, her constant compromising of the truth, and frequent nightmares.

She never seemed to have the time or ability to enjoy being a Mom. For her, vacation was a time of fantasy, not relaxation. It was a place to pretend everything was okay. Returning home always seemed to be a "dread" for her – because awaiting her was more fear and stress.

I'm happy to tell you, she's no longer in our family – something happened one day that forced her to leave. Was I sad? Do we miss her? No. Actually, her leaving was a great blessing for our whole family.

**Wait! AM I INSANE or HATEFUL for saying so?
Before you put the book down,
please let me explain...**

You see, that was the old Lisa. Today, it's as if I'm another woman. Looking back at old videos is as if I'm watching another human being. Someone I once knew, but who is now gone. Although she's gone and forever changed, each time I see the old videos, my heart is filled with sadness for her and all the women who are in pain like I was. Behind those eyes was hopelessness, pain, fear, and stress that is simply not here today. Jesus is the only one that can bring a change like that!

Still today, tears well up in my eyes for all the "Lisa's" that are still out there, that are locked up in the prison I was once in. The "Lisa's" that are desperately screaming inside for help, but are walking around in hopelessness, not knowing how to get free and stay free!

The "Lisa's" that are good people, who may even go to church regularly, but who are emotionally and spiritually bleeding to death inside. Those who are full of fear and self-hatred, who no matter how slim or heavy, always feel fat, ugly, or not good enough. Those who have tried everything: counseling, conferences, hospitals, drugs, friends, careers and still feel they'll never be anything more than they are today. My heart goes out to the women that are tired of trying, performing, pretending, or striving. Who are always looking for something new to make them feel better about who they are as a wife, daughter, mother, friend, sister, and woman of God.

I'm talking today to the women that are looking desperately for the key to get out of the cage and be FREE once and for all! Free from the pain, free from the anxiety, depression, and fear – and free to be who they REALLY ARE in CHRIST.

Sure, I found many temporary fixes – and you can too. The most frequent ones for me were not drugs or alcohol, but shopping sprees, cigarettes, trying to be perfect. Every 'fix' outside of Jesus, is our drug or idol. For me, each one of these led me deeper and deeper until there was no place else to go, but deeper into the pit of debt and despair. I think the most deceptive idols are the ones that look "good" to us. Such as "being a good person."

The serpent (the enemy) convinced Eve of this in the garden of Eden. It is the tree of the Knowledge of Good and Evil that is still one of his greatest lures to us, today. Satan knows that deep down, we want to be counted as "good". But the only thing that will bring true righteousness and salvation, is our faith in God's grace to forgive us through the shed blood of Jesus. This is the power in the tree of Life – it's the Spirit of Life that sets us free - Jesus. To believe in the one that God sent to save us, takes real faith! Out of that freedom comes the true, pure motive to do all to obey our Father in gratitude for His mercy upon us. Our good works, could never earn us right standing with God. There's nothing wrong with being a good person, unless that is our way of earning our salvation, or substituting it for spending time with God and "knowing Him in a deep and personal way". God desires our friendship.

What is it for you today? Your career? Friends? Being busy? Books & Knowledge? The internet? Projects? Church stuff or religion? Clothes? Being "Super-Mom"? Or being a good person? Sex, alcohol or drugs? Are all of these things wrong? Not unless you substitute them for Jesus and are trying to fill the void in your life with them.

Do you use any of these things to drown yourself so you don't have to think about the pain, or the hole in your heart? What do you use to try to fill that unsatisfiable place in your life? If it's spending time in God's presence every day, you're on the right track. If not, today is the best day to get things right with Him.

If it's anything other than the living Jesus – I pray you will wake up today and realize, it's an idol. It's deception, and a trap of the enemy that will keep you locked up and in PRISON. And it's 100% hopelessly unsatisfying!

You see, I was a church attender who was raised in a Spirit-filled, bible believing church. I knew God's word and could quote it at random. I was a good person, had good health, a beautiful home, furniture, car, awesome husband who loved me, and a beautiful little baby boy that I was privileged to stay at home with and raise. I was a size 5, had a regular vacation and lots of friends. But…

I had no peace – and was hurting inside!

I was a shell filled with pain and misery - a walking "open-wound." "How could this happen", you ask? "Especially after growing up in a good church, with men and women of God who led it". Knowing the word of God, and being raised by a Christian Mom is not enough. Through all of this pain, I led Bible studies, sang in church for special musicals, and talked to people about the truths of God's word. None of that will bring you peace or deep inner healing and freedom. None of these will bring you freedom from fear and bondage. Only JESUS can!

THE TURNING POINT

JESUS! Yes, Jesus gives us a crown of beauty for ashes, and a garment of praise instead of a spirit of despair (Isaiah 61:3). He takes the precious from the vile (Jeremiah 15:9). Instead of shame, He gives us a double portion. Instead of disgrace, we are then able to rejoice in our inheritance. In Him, everlasting joy is ours (Isaiah 61:7).

WHAT WAS THE TURNING POINT? God had already begun to pull at my heart by helping me realize how lost, miserable, and powerless I really was. I couldn't take it anymore. I began to pray something I never prayed before. Something happened inside me that led me to pray a *radical prayer*. I was ready for GOD TO CHANGE ME, for REAL!

"Take my life and literally CHANGE ME", I cried. "Change me or kill me, God – because I just can't take this anymore. I hate me and who I am, God. I don't want to wreck my husband or future children's lives. I'm tired of running to you only when I want something, Lord. Please make me faithful to you, and bring me back to the place I need to be in you, Lord. I want you to use me and make me faithful to you."

EVERYONE HAS AN
END TO THEIR ROPE

God has a way to reach every heart! Just before this prayer, the credit card debt and despair had created more pressure than I could handle. We had gotten out of debt once, and within 6 months, had completely gotten ourselves back into the same pit of debt that we were in previously. The bills were too much to handle, and it looked like we were headed for bankruptcy. You have to understand, I grew up in a home without a Dad and on government food stamps. At that point in my life, filing bankruptcy was like a prison sentence to me. It was like sending me back to my poverty-stricken childhood.

Yet, God was already working his plan to do something mighty in my life! He is indeed in control! He knows how to reach each and every one of us, doesn't He? This was the hook that God used to reel me into Himself with. He turned my need and fear into the bait that hooked and tugged at my hungry heart. No one fishes as well as Jesus! I was about to learn that He never gives up on us, and is full of love, power, and mercy! Within six months after I began praying that, God had already done a mighty work to change me, but something extra-ordinary happened one day. I received a phone call that changed my life forever.

THE PHONE CALL THAT CHANGED MY LIFE

The phone rang one bright early morning. It was 6 am. It was my little praying Mom who phoned from her apartment in Florida. When I heard her voice, I knew something had happened, there was something urgent in her voice. I listened intently.

"Lisa," she blurted out, "I've been pacing the floor since 4 am, waiting for it to get late enough to call you." She had my full attention. She continued, "I was awakened about 4 am with you on my mind, so I started praying for you, and my prayers turned into weeping for you. This went on for quite a while, then, the Lord spoke to me about you."

"ME, " I said, startled!? "Almighty God spoke to YOU about me?" Though she was a prayer warrior, I never, remember her saying God SPOKE TO HER ABOUT ME personally, before. Curiosity was about to explode in my heart and mind.

"Well," she said, "though it was only 4 words, they impressed my heart so strongly that I walked the floor for almost 2 hours waiting to call you. I know God wants me to tell you this, " she added.

"What were the words, Mom", I asked, "what did He say"?

She responded,

"He said, 'Lisa's running from Me'".

INSTANTLY it felt as if a pent up dam broke inside me and tears poured from my eyes that puddled onto the kitchen counter. I had never so suddenly and violently begun to weep in all of my life. It came from deep within me. I was weeping so hard and violently, I bent over and fell to my knees on the kitchen floor. I wept uncontrollably for more than 5 minutes, while Mom sat there on the phone waiting and praying.

It felt like a dam had broken inside my heart. The anointing and weight of TRUTH and the presence of God that was in her words broke through. In that moment, they were the most beautiful, truthful, and powerful words I had heard in all my life. It felt equivalent to a nuclear bomb exploding in my life. You see, only God knew that for months I had been praying and crying out to Him with my whole heart to be changed. I asked Him to show me what was wrong with me. I had been asking Him to show me what the root of the problem was in my life and why I had been unable to be faithful to Him."

The greatest revelation to me that day was not only that I had my answer. It was also that "Almighty God" had been listening to my prayers! I mean REALLY listening to me!

WHEN DARKNESS TURNS TO DAWN

For the first time since I was a small child, I did not feel alone. Something powerful was happening in my life. Something big! This whole experience confirmed it to me. With those four words came HOPE as big as the sun. It burst forth in my heart, like the dawn breaking forth after the longest, dark night of my life.

The dark night of my soul,
had been invaded by the pure light of God's
goodness and mercy.

You see, for years I had been convinced of something which locked me in the darkest pit of hopelessness I had ever known – it was the lie from satan that I had traveled too far from God. It was the lie that I was too dirty, sinful, and bad for God to take me back. I was convinced that God would never have anything to do with me again. You see, I was called into ministry at age 10. But at age seventeen, this once pure hearted young woman had willingly turned her back on a Holy All-Powerful God, and His love. While I was gone, I had feasted on all that the world had offered me. How could a HOLY GOD, ever look again upon a rebellious child who willingly turned her back on His goodness and chose to check out the wild side? Before this phone call, I was convinced I was too far gone, and had no chance of ever being near My Heavenly Father, again.

Where are you today? Are you away from Him, like I had been? Are you wandering? Or are you too, finding yourself curious about the other side? Or have you too, wandered so far that you've lost hope that you could ever be completely sold out to Him, again? Or maybe you've never known what it is to be so in love with Him that He is the reason for your peace and joy. No matter where you are today, the truth is, He's longing for you to turn and run to Him with all of your heart. He waits for us to set aside our substitute gods, the things we use to drug ourselves with and just run to Him. The truth is, He is the perfect prodigal Father.

**"The chariots of God are tens of thousands
and thousands of thousands;
the Lord has come from Sinai into his sanctuary.
When you ascended on high,
You led captives in your train,
You received gifts from men,
even from the rebellious –
that you, O Lord God,**

might dwell there.
Praise be to the Lord, to God our Savior,
who daily bears our burdens."
Our God is a God who saves;
from the Sovereign Lord
comes escape from death."
Psalm 68:17-20

Still weeping on the phone, I finally gathered myself together enough to utter sounds that were barely understandable. Gathering my crumbled up tissues, I managed to mutter, "Yes, Mom, - I have been running from God. But I don't know why. Why, Mom? Why have I been running from Him?"

With tears and gentle strength, she responded, "I don't know honey, but I see you trying to collect and buy things to make yourself happy, it's as if nothing is enough for you – I don't know why you feel you need all those things you are constantly buying."

"You're right," I cried (more calmly, now), "but how do I stop running from Him, Mom? How do I find my way back to the place I once was in Him, Mom?"

She replied, "I don't know, honey, but God knows, and He will lead you". Little did I know, the fact that I had been crying out to Him for months to change me, was indeed part of my journey back "home" into His loving, merciful arms. It was His immeasurable loving heart breaking forth through my mother's prayers of intercession – that was causing me to be drawn back to Him again!

What if she hadn't yielded to God's leading and didn't cry out to Him for me during the 10 years

that I was so busy running from Him?
What if she had given up?

This is good fruit produced through Kingdom-living. It released the Divine power that I needed to change in my life. Moms who minister are anointed with the same Holy Spirit that Jesus was. They are anointed by God to set the captives free, to speak spirit-filled words of Life from heaven that sustain the weary, heal broken hearts, and in the Name of Jesus, are used by God to change lives and reveal His glory. God desires to use every Mom in the universe that will yield to Him, to snatch souls from the fire, and to restore and change lives.

A PRAYER OF THANKS
FOR PRAYING MOMS

How I Thank You,
My Gracious and Merciful Father,
for a praying Mom.
One that was willing to pace the floors
in the middle of the night
and cry out to you for me.
One that was willing to carry the burden
of your heart ~
the return of my lost and broken soul.
You used her to pray me back in from
out of the darkness,
To enable me to return to the light of your glory.

You used her to speak words of life to this helpless
and broken vessel.

~ ~ ~ ~ ~

I know, Lord, that it was Jesus IN her
not only being my caretaker,
but an intercessor and minister of your amazing
grace to my spirit and soul.
Forever, I Thank You for your perfect love
and for her life, her service,
and her sacrifice unto you.

~ ~ ~ ~ ~ ~

Now, Father, please help each of us...
and especially those who have
never had such a gift,
learn from this example and
do the same for those you have entrusted to us.
Teach us to pray, Lord.
By your grace, I pray you will do the work of the
ministry through us, Lord.
In Jesus Name, Amen.

"For God did not send his Son into the world
to condemn the world but to
save the world through him.
Whoever believes in him is not condemned,
but whoever does not believe stands condemned
already because he has not believed in the
name of God's one and only Son.

John 3:17-18

nine

Lifting the Veil
Of Deception

"To the Jews who believed him, Jesus said, 'If you hold to my
teaching, you are really my disciples.
Then you will know the truth,
and the truth shall set you free.'"
John 8:31b, 32

*T*he *Mom Ministry* is about walking in *freedom* in Christ. In this chapter, with the help of the Holy Spirit, I am going to glorify Jesus as my "Deliverer". The phone call, I spoke of earlier, changed my life and began a chain reaction of supernatural circumstances for me. During the next season of my life, God continued to reveal Himself through orchestrated events that led me to another life changing experience. One of these took place a short time after the phone call that I spoke of in the earlier chapter. It was a weekend that radically changed me! If you've been seeking Him with all of your heart for something powerful, He has something MIGHTY for you, as well.

I returned home from this particular life changing weekend with four explosive things:

1. An excitement and love for Jesus that I had never imagined was possible.

2. A daily passion to worship Him with everything that is within me.

3. A determination to use my life to get 'even' with the enemy for robbing me for so long.

4. An unsatisfiable desire to give my life away to see every bound human being in the world set free!

I came home from that weekend singing songs of joy and freedom, while speaking words filled with faith, hope, and love. After returning home, my sister Linda, took one look at me and said, "You're different, Lisa. What happened to you?! I saw something different in you from the moment you walked in the door. What happened to you?"

She was right! I was filled with such joy and zeal, it effected every area of my life. People that knew me recognized a change even in my physical countenance. A "phone ministry" began immediately. Everyone that called was somehow impacted by this incredible experience in my life. Since that weekend, everywhere I go, I love to tell what Jesus did for me.

I knew that if Jesus could set ME free, He could set anyone free, and that's what I began to tell everyone. It doesn't matter what you are bound to, today. It doesn't matter how **long** you've been bound – the Name of Jesus is above every name! He's eagerly waiting to bring deliverance to every captive that seeks Him!

THE PROOF IS IN THE FRUIT

I call that weekend, "My Miracle Weekend". I came home that weekend changed forever.

It was Jesus Himself who used an anointed man and woman of God that spoke to a group of women at a women's retreat. JESUS met me there, and SET ME FREE. This couple was anointed to prophesy, preach the gospel of freedom, restoration, healing, and deliverance to every hungry heart that was open to receive! Every word in Isaiah 61 hit my life in full force. It ignited an eruption of divine power that consumed me, and changed my life and family forever.

Upon my return home that weekend, my son, Andrew (a toddler at the time) said, "Mommy? You are different." As small as he was, and as little as his natural mind could comprehend, his spirit recognized the new and explosive freedom and power that was brought into our home! Yes, "Jesus changed Mommy"!

And friend, God wants to do something new and mighty in you! God's word says He does not show favoritism. He is the same yesterday, today and forever. It may be in your motherhood, marriage, or ministry. The power of God consuming YOU will bring change to every area of your life.

As the Holy Spirit brings HOPE to you today, reach out with the hands of your heart and take hold of it. And say, "Yes, Lord – as you have done for Lisa and her family, do it for ME and MY FAMILY". Cry out and don't stop until you GET YOUR MIRACLE!

If you too have been "locked up" in one or more areas in your life, God has a plan for you, too! It's a plan to unlock you – transform you – empower you – and use you to bring Him great glory! He desires to set you free from everything that holds you and your children back. As you cry out to Him, He will direct you on your personal and unique path to freedom and deliverance.

THE PATH TO FREEDOM

For months prior to this experience, the Lord saw me pacing the floor crying out for a miracle. I walked and prayed, and prayed and walked. When my little one was down for a nap, I walked around the house and cried out time and time again, "God, I don't know what I need, but there's something wrong with me. Please, God, help me - give me a miracle - I want to be happy and all that you want me to be." Many times I'd wake up in the middle of the night to go read the bible and pray, "Lord, please, lead me to what I need – I don't even know what to ask for – but I know You know what I need." When I was driving to the grocery store, I would pray and cry, sometimes weep, "Lord, why am I still not happy inside, I know you are doing something in my life, helping me not run from you anymore, but MORE, Lord, I want MORE. I want you to consume me and take me, completely.

Change me MORE, Lord.   Don't stop what you are doing in me, Father..."

Each moment I cried out, Jesus was leading me closer to my freedom. God was using my prayers to move and position me to receive my hearts desire. The key is to not stop seeking Him UNTIL you receive! And then, we must continue to seek Him, after. I didn't know it, but each prayer and earnest cry filled a bowl of fragrant incense in the heavens to my Loving Heavenly Father. My dear friend, Lori, put it like this, "when we weep before Him, Jesus is there with us, sitting or kneeling at our side, cupping His hands and catching our tears."

When the bowl of my tears and prayers reached it's capacity, it released something from heaven that was poured into my life. His divine power washed over me and carried me to my deliverance from satan's hold! There's something powerful and unimaginable about "seeking the Lord." God designed this process in such a way, that it does things deep within our spirit that are too big for our mind to comprehend. I believe in those moments, He is digging deep wells in our heart to hold the water of His spirit. It's safe to let go of our emotions in His presence. As we pour out our hearts before Him, He fills us with His heart.

I'm telling you, sisters, God has commissioned me to write these words today ~ to share with you the truth and hope, that if you too have been seeking Him, and crying out for something powerful from Him for you and your family, He will answer your heart cries too! You're on your way! Let me encourage you today to keep going! Don't settle for what you get in church on Sunday, there's MORE. Seek Him for EVERYTHING He has for you and your family every day of the week!

It's part of God's ministry to Moms. His plan is that we may truly be "Moms who Minister"!

Jesus is here to anoint your head with the oil of gladness that comes from having every chain broken that has bound your family in oppression and captivity!

"I cried out to God for help;
I cried out to God to hear me.
When I was in distress, I sought the Lord;
at night I stretched out untiring hands
And my soul refused to be comforted.
I remembered you, O God, and I groaned;
I mused, and my spirit grew faint...
Then I thought, "To this I will appeal:
the years of the right hand of the Most High."
I will remember the deeds of the Lord;
Yes, I will remember your miracles of long ago,
I will meditate on all your works and
consider all your mighty deeds.
With your mighty arm you redeemed your people
the descendants of Jacob and Joseph...
your path led through the sea,
your way through the mighty waters,
though your footprints were not seen.
You led your people like a flock by the hand
of Moses and Aaron."
Psalm 77:1-3, 10-12, 15, 19-20

According to scripture, if you are a believer, God is ready to set you free to be on fire with His light and glory! And though His footprints are unseen, verse 19 in the passage above says, He is leading you to fill your hungering heart with His love, freedom, and spirit. He is doing this so that Isaiah 61 can come alive in your household!

BOUND UP CHRISTIANS

Why is this truth so important for every believer to understand? Because the Bible says, satan is out to kill, steal, and destroy. It doesn't say that once we get saved the battle is over. The truth is, it has only begun. However, the battle keeps us climbing higher on the Mountain of the Lord. The enemy fights tooth and nail to keep us ignorant and unable to fully break free. He knows the more ignorant and bound we stay, the less damage we can do to his kingdom!

That's why God has given us the full armor of God and the ministry of deliverance in the body of Christ. To victoriously stand against the enemy and build the Kingdom of God! He's given us spiritual weapons to defeat the enemy in every area of our life. But we must realize that they are needed, learn how to use them, and then teach our children. A Mom who ministers, seeks for her freedom from the Lord, and is then used by God to minister to others. It's God's plan of multiplication and fruit bearing. Liberating captives is a normal, healthy function of the New Testament Church.

If you have come to believe and know the Truth, that Jesus is your Savior and the only way to the Father. The Bible says, the devil has lost his power to condemn you. John 3:18 teaches us that you are no longer condemned.

This makes you and your children a serious threat to the darkness. As you learn to walk in freedom, and God's power, the enemy knows you will drive him out of every place God sends you. This is why we undergo such great opposition and trials after we are born again! He wants to stop and immobilize you from fulfilling the plan of God for your life. If he can't stop you, he'll hurl every possible distraction at you to delay you or lead you into complacency.

RESTORATION AND DELIVERANCE?

I'm grateful to God for the ministry of deliverance. Our Jesus is a God of mercy. This ministry is a part of His work through the Holy Spirit.

Deliverance is not a scary or spooky thing. It's Jesus' love and mercy to the captives. God uses spirit-filled vessels, but it's the Holy Spirit through those vessels who actually performs the work. He is the same, yesterday, today, and forever. What He did in the Book of Acts, He is still doing today. And He wants to use us all to bring our Heavenly Father glory.

We receive a new spirit within us when we become born again (Titus 3:5). Sometimes though, the soul (our mind, will, and emotions), can still be bound by oppressive spirits. This is a sign that inner healing and deliverance is necessary. These spirits can hinder us and hold us back from fully walking in obedience, faith, and the fullness of the joy that we have in Christ.

Such spirits can include: rejection, infirmity, unworthiness, hatred, addiction, (all of which can enter or come to oppress you through traumatic experiences in your life), and many others. Deep wounds, trauma, abuse, and devastating life experiences can open doors for the enemy to enter or weigh us down and control us if we do not forgive or move successfully through the grief and healing process.

One by one, as we are set free in these areas, the word of God must then be used to build walls of righteousness and truth around our mind. This is so that we may dwell in and operate out of a mind and heart that is filled with His grace, truth, and faith!

There is some controversy in the body of Christ today about whether a Christian can be possessed or oppressed. The bottom line is, whether the enemy is IN a Christian or ON a Christian – let's just get people free, help them stay free, and teach people how to help others get set free! The harvest is too big, and time is too short! When delivering the captives, Jesus didn't stop to ask such questions. He simply moved in the power of the Holy Spirit to free every captive desiring freedom.

HOW DO I KNOW IF I NEED DELIVERANCE?

Each situation is unique. That's why we must rely upon the Holy Spirit to reveal and lead us through our path to deliverance, healing, and restoration. In my particular case, as I continued in prayer, I kept sensing that there was something wrong with me, but I couldn't put my finger on it. Because of this, I didn't know which questions to ask to get the help that I needed. I truly didn't know how to describe what I felt inside. Because I was unaware that there was a ministry called 'deliverance" in the body of Christ, I didn't know to go to someone with this type of wisdom or anointing. But I DID know that Jesus was aware of all I needed – so I asked Him to continue to lead me to what He knew I needed.   And HE DID!   He is so wonderful! He wants us free and healthy, even more than we do! The Holy Spirit is faithful to lead us and guide us as we continue to seek Him until we receive our break through.

I have come to learn this, though:
Many times, continual lack of victory in particular areas of our character and personality, are caused by one of two things:

1) Either it is an area in our life that still needs growth or maturity through studying and obeying the word, or,

2) Inner Healing or Deliverance is needed.
(In this case prophetic counseling is advised, or the aid of experienced deliverance ministry)

In many Christians, though they love the Lord and are saved, there are still places deep within that are in need of healing and freedom.   This was so in my case.   Here are some examples that might indicate this sort of counseling or ministry is needed:

Uncontrolled fits of rage, continued battles with paralyzing fear, voices that tell you to do wrong (hurt yourself or others), chronic depression, inability to have healthy relationships with most people, compulsive shyness, continued "tape recording" typed memories of painful or traumatic incidents (that happened long ago), continued heaviness, confusion, mental illness, uncontrolled compulsive behaviors, addictions.

Having some of these symptoms is no need for alarm or fear!   The Holy Spirit is faithful to lead and nudge us continuously about steps He wants us to take. He knows whether or not we need deliverance. Ask Him to confirm whether or not you need inner healing or deliverance, and he will!

DELIVERANCE IS FOR REAL, AND FOR TODAY!

Unlike Jesus, the enemy is a deceiver and likes to mask himself. He works hard to make us think "it's just us," or "we're imagining it". I know there are many in the body of Christ today who do not believe in deliverance ministry – but that did not stop me from pursuing my freedom and inner healing. Not all need deliverance ministry, but it's important that we embrace and respect this work of the Holy Spirit in the body of Christ for those who DO need it.

I was so ignorant about deliverance, I thought it was only for "Full Gospel, Charismatic, or really wild churches". I also thought that healing was mostly for giant crusades or mostly found on the foreign mission field. But God began to open my eyes to the reality and truth that the Word of God and all that it offers the body of Christ is for today and for the body of Christ as a whole. I am so grateful He opened my heart and mind to the fact that He wanted to use the power of the Holy Spirit to "deliver me." In a short time, I didn't care anymore if everyone didn't believe in it. The RADICAL and AWESOME CHANGE in my life speaks for itself! I remember wanting desperately to be free and joyful, and the day came, when Jesus did it!

Jesus used the ministry of healing and deliverance to "help restore me and catapult me forward into the purpose of God for my life"!   I still praise Him for it! Deliverance is an act of God's love and mercy to the captives! That is why in the Holy of Holies, His Presence rested upon the "Mercy Seat." He IS merciful to all those who seek to know Him, love Him, and worship Him!

Those who don't believe deliverance or healing is Godly or for today, can't receive from this ministry. Not all believed it during Jesus' day, either. The truth is, everything in the Kingdom of God comes through faith and believing God's word.   Kenneth E. Hagin once said, "We can't receive if we don't believe, and if we have received, it's because we've believed"![v]

> **"...how God anointed Jesus of Nazareth with the**
> **Holy Spirit and power, and how**
> **He went about doing good, and healing**
> **all who were under the power of the devil,**
> **because God was with him."**
> **Acts 10:38**

Unbelief disqualifies us from receiving all that God has for us! I chose instead, to trust the Lord as He led me. I trusted that He loved me and would not lead or steer me into danger. I followed peace and looked for confirmations to ensure it was Jesus doing the leading. This protected me from being deceived in an area of the gospel that was new to me.   Jesus will do the same for you and your children, dear sister.

FEAR OF DELIVERANCE

It's important that you understand that satan does not want you free or healed. The enemy attacks us in areas we do not have understanding in. But as we grow in faith and understanding of God's ways, the enemy loses the ability to attack us and succeed. The devil will hurl every lying, doubtful, fearful, unbelieving thought at you to try to stop you from receiving your miracle, deliverance, and freedom.

The enemy hates deliverance and healing ministry. Why? The devil wants us to stay bound and sick. Because He knows the freer and more healthy we become inwardly and outwardly, the more strength we will exert towards advancing the Kingdom of God. He knows that as we press in to be whole – we will touch the hem of Jesus garment and our pain will be transformed into a ministry!

It's time, Moms - we must decide to press in and break free in every area of our lives! Our children need a Mom that is whole, walking in joy, victory, and divine health and freedom!

One woman shared that though the Lord led her to see that she needed some deliverance and inner healing, she was afraid of being embarrassed by what might be said, or what It might look like. She was nervous about what kind of spirit might come out, or how evil the spirit that had held her captive was. But as she prayed and continued to obey the Lord in His direction to pursue deliverance, the Lord led her to a ministry that was right for her. She was NOT embarrassed or humiliated – but set FREE in a loving and victorious way! Today she is free and moving forward in her calling!

I learned that related spirits come to attack and oppress our mind to the point where we can be paralyzed or immobilized from living a healthy Christian life.

A spirit-filled believer, leader, or minister who is skilled and experienced in deliverance, will be able to help you distinguish the source of the problem. I have enclosed a helpful resource list for further research and study if you desire to research this ministry further. Seeking the counsel of those skilled in these areas can be very helpful. Pray and obey the Lord – move forward in faith, not fear – Jesus is kind and knows what you need. In Psalm 23: 2, 3 David prayed, "

**"He makes me lie down in green pastures,
he leads me beside quiet waters,**

He restores my soul..."

BE CAREFUL TO KEEP IT BALANCED!

Every challenge we face is not demonic. Most struggles and battles we face each day can be overcome by continual and uncompromising obedience to God's word. It's easy to begin blaming our daily struggles with our flesh on the enemy. It's important to learn that all difficulties are not due to demonic oppression.

Does deliverance remove every obstacle from our path? No. Jesus freed me from the enemy that kept me from walking in peace with God and man. But, God still had to continue to teach me how to walk in His ways on a daily basis. Every day is part of God's plan to complete the work that He began in us.

HOW DO YOU KNOW if you need deliverance? Pray, read the word, seek counsel, and most of all - ask God to show you if deliverance is needed. Stay as close to the Lord as possible. He will confirm it and as you ask Him to He will lead you to a skilled, pure-hearted servant, who is equipped and able to pray for you to receive what you need.

THERE'S A PURPOSE FOR YOUR FREEDOM

Your inheritance and life's purpose have been paid for in full by the blood of Jesus. It includes joy, peace, health, restoration of your relationships, children, marriage, time and ministry. All of this began to come as I sought Jesus with all my heart on a continual basis. The Holy Spirit drew me through prayer and His word.

Through my ignorance of the enemy's schemes, he was able to rob me of many years of peace and purpose in my life and family – until the Lord brought the reality and power of deliverance into my life. Jesus brought the light that exposed the enemy and dispelled the darkness. He is not only our Savior, but also our Deliverer.

Can Christians be demonically attacked and oppressed? Yes. My life is living proof. Though I confessed Jesus as Lord for many years, satan had successfully held me captive in areas of my mind, will, and emotions, through deception. And until I prayed and asked God for a miracle – I was bound and unable to see lasting change in my Christian walk and Motherhood. As I sought the Lord, wanting to be made whole, He had already planned *The Mom Ministry* for me. But first, He had to lead me through my path of deliverance. What He does for us – God wants to do for others, as well.

"Go into all the world and preach the good news
to all creation. Whoever believes and is baptized
will be saved, but whoever does not believe will
be condemned. And these signs will accompany
those who believe:
In my name they will drive out demons; they will
speak in new tongues; they will pick up snakes
with their hands; and when they drink deadly
poison, it will not hurt them at all; they will place
their hands on sick people,
and they will get well."
Mark 16:15-18

Thank God for the truth and power that sets us free. Today, Jesus is alive and well, still setting the captives free. It may be time to reread Isaiah 61, again, and also remember David's words in Psalms: "He restoreth my soul"…

"Thank you, Jesus, for restoring those who seek
you and open their heart to believe and receive
deliverance from the enemies grip –
oh what love and mercy you have for us
every day, Lord.
We are grateful and thank you".

CHILDREN AND
DELIVERANCE

I received a call one morning from a young Christian woman named, Ann. "Lisa", she said, "my daughter, who is 7 years old is in serious trouble, and she needs prayer. I don't know what to do. Can you help?"

After listening to her story, she explained that her daughter was depressed and was suicidal after returning home from her Dad's house (they were divorced). She explained that her daughter had been in a horrible mood from the time Ann had picked her up in the car. Her daughter's conversation with her in the car was difficult. Within minutes she sensed that something more was going on that was deeply wrong. The conversation unnecessarily escalated and spun out of control when her daughter began saying things like, "I hate myself...I wish I were dead". Ann's daughter began to cry and tried to open the car door to jump out numerous times as they were driving down the Express Way. She was going to jump out. "I just don't want to live anymore, Mom," she cried. Ann, frightened and shaken up, phoned as soon as she arrived home.

I prayed with her and asked the Lord for wisdom. The Lord prompted us to ask her little girl if she would be willing to talk to me on the phone. She agreed, and as I spoke with her, the Lord confirmed to our spirit that she needed deliverance prayer. He then prompted me to encourage her tenderly by sharing how I felt as a young child of divorce and how depressed I used to get. I shared with her that I truly needed someone to see how much prayer and help I needed. After asking her if she wanted me to come and pray with her, I got in the car to drive over. As I drove I began to intercede.

It took about 45 minutes to arrive where this precious little seven year old was waiting. But she was waiting with something in her hand that was more precious to me than gold. As I was driving to her house, she drew for me a small picture of a heart and wrote on it, "Thank You, Lisa." She was expecting to receive from God. So much so, she had already prepared her "Thank You gift" ahead of time!

This spoke volumes to my heart. Though she was only 7 years old and didn't understand a lot of what was really going on, she knew enough to know that she was in trouble, needed prayer, and that she was going to receive something great from God when we prayed. This is the FAITH that God wants each of us to operate in. I keep this little thank you note inside the first page of the Book of Acts in my Bible as a reminder of what Jesus will do for an open willing heart. It reminds me that we are indeed the modern day, "Acts Church".

This precious little girl knew she had a need that only Jesus could meet. Thus, she had prepared her THANK YOU gift with a heart full of expectancy and gratitude! She believed in the power of Jesus to help her and was set free!

"and a little child shall lead them"
Isaiah 11:6b

What an example to the Body of Christ! We talked a little and then quietly began to pray together with her Mom. In a matter of a few moments, the spirit of suicide and rejection left this little girls body. Condemnation was nowhere to be found, but was replaced with freedom, righteousness, and joy in the Holy Spirit.   Her Mom and I felt these spirits left simultaneously and quietly. Suddenly, this precious little one's face lit up the room as she began to sigh very loudly and say,

**"I feel so much better now,
I feel so much lighter and free."**

There was no doubt in each of our minds that Jesus had truly shown up and done something powerful for her that day. She will never forget it.

Today she is growing up to love the Lord and serve Him by traveling on Kid's missions trips (determined to make an impact for Jesus). Yes, Jesus touches the children and delivers them from the enemy, as well!

WHAT I DIDN'T KNOW
WAS HURTING ME

I'm out to expose the enemy today! Expose the fact that the devil has a voice! And he speaks to every human being that will listen to his lies – CHRISTIANS, TOO! I'm not saying this to glorify him, but to expose him.

For many years, not knowing this kept me locked up in thinking it was my own voice that I was listening to. Satan had literally convinced me that I was going crazy. I had even battled off thoughts of suicide at times. For years I kept thinking, "if I am a Christian, how can I be thinking these things, what's wrong with me? Why can't I just be normal"?

You see, I grew up believing there was a devil, but I didn't know he spoke thoughts or suggestions into my mind. Therefore, I was listening to his lies for years thinking it was my own accusing thoughts about myself.

He would constantly whisper condemning, fearful and hateful thoughts to me. Things such as, "I don't want to go to that 'get together', they probably won't like me anyway." Or, "nobody likes me." "I can't do it, it's just too hard." "I'll never be as good as she is...", "I'll never be good enough for anything or anyone."

God first had to set me free from the lying spirits that were always working to torment me. Then, I needed to learn how to keep the enemy closed out of my mind and life. After Jesus opened the jail cell door and exposed the enemy as a liar in my life, God began to show me the truth about who I really was in Christ. Jesus, in all His love, then took scripture and spoke it directly into my heart. This changed me from the inside out! For the first time, I was able to believe that I was something special to God! The self-hatred and lying thoughts blew away as if they were never there! Jesus taught me that I wasn't a piece of junk, and that by His shed blood, He made me worthy to come to Him and be God's daughter! He taught me that I am His beautiful bride, "His delight", whom he loves more than His own life. His spoken words to our heart are truly THAT powerful!

After He did this, He began to teach me how to use the armor and spiritual weapons He gave me. He taught me about three different voices, to help me distinguish between His voice and the enemies. He did this so that I could give the devil "the boot" each time he tries to come near and lure me away again.

Today, I'd like to share this valuable teaching with you. Coming to understand this, made me much stronger and able to walk victoriously.

WHICH VOICE IS WHICH?

There are three voices that can be heard speaking to us. Only two of these voices are what we want to be listening to.

1) The voice of the Holy Spirit – If it doesn't sound like your loving Heavenly Father speaking to you, reject it immediately. Conviction in his voice, compels us to pray and repent which leads to freedom. There is love and clarity in His voice. Peace always comes after. Elijah heard His voice in the wind. Samuel heard His voice in the quiet night. God speaks to us in our heart, gut, or belly. You may sense, see, or hear something. If it's God, He'll confirm it, more than 2 or 3 times.

    The Bible says, the voice of the Lord is like a still small voice, and can be heard by waiting quietly in His presence. Make time to wait upon Him during prayer and worship. He will also illuminate scripture to you as you read His word. This often feels like the words are coming off the page.

2) <u>Our own voice</u> - our thoughts, mind, and imagination.

3) <u>The voice of the enemy / demons</u> – can sound like your own voice in your head. Always look for the fruit of the thought or suggestion. The fruit of the enemy's voice will produce confusion, fear, doubt, worry, anxiousness, tension, panic, condemnation, depression, and others. It may feel like these spirits are speaking from the outside in. The enemy will always lead us away from obedience to God's word and try to push us out of God's timing.

4) <u>Not sure?</u>   Write it down, pray on it, seek counsel from a wise, seasoned, spirit-filled leader.   A dear "Church Mom" of mine, Pat, once taught me something I'll never forget. I've used this tid-bit of wise advice perhaps more than any other I've received. She said, *"when you're not SURE what to do – do nothing, except, wait and pray until you DO know what to do. Then and only then, move forward."*

The Holy Spirit's voice will NEVER tell you to do something contrary to the Word of God.

As believers, we must study to know the Word of God, and learn to distinguish the difference between our voice, the enemy's voice, and the voice of the

Holy Spirit. When we recognize it is the enemy at the onset, we can resist him immediately before he is able to get a foothold in our thoughts.

Since Jesus set me free, each day in prayer, I apply the blood of Jesus over my mind and spiritual ears. This protects my thoughts from the enemy. I then began to fill my mind and speech with words that are edifying and full of faith in God's goodness. We can then choose to quickly obey the voice of the Holy Spirit and resist the enemy.   Hesitancy to obey, or disobedience to the Lord causes our spiritual ears and senses to be dulled.   This is dangerous, and if we continue to do so, our heart will continue to harden. We will then be unable to hear the Lord or sense Him speaking to us.

Ask the Holy Spirit, the Spirit of Truth, to give you discernment and help you grow in understanding in this area. I John 4 speaks in great detail about the need we have, as the body of Christ, to test the spirits and be able to discern the difference between what is truly God's direction. We are warned many times by Jesus to not be deceived (to be wise as serpents, but gentle as doves). We avoid deception by, "being lovers of the truth", and staying close to Jesus, "the Good Shepherd". John 10:25-28 says,

**"Jesus answered, "I did tell you, but you do not believe. The miracles I do in my Father's name speak for me, but you do not believe because you are not my sheep. My sheep listen to my voice, I know them, and they follow me.
I give them eternal life, and they shall never perish; no one can snatch them out of my hand."**

HE'S AFTER YOUR "MOM MINISTRY"

While we are covered in discouragement, or depression, we can be immobilized from praying prayers of faith, and worshipping God. The truth is, for almost 30 years of my life, satan had me locked up in a prison of lies in my mind. So are many others.

In the chapter entitled, "The Power to Change", I described the young woman that I used to be. Yes, I had come to believe that Jesus was Lord as a young child, but had been unable to experience full freedom. Yes, my sins had been forgiven, but I had other issues that needed addressing, as well. I had been sexually abused starting at age 3, and verbally and physically abused, also. This left open doors in my life for insecurity, self-hatred, severe depression, suicide, and shame. 2 years of counseling helped a little, but didn't bring any lasting change, peace, or break through.

My Mom and Dad were separated when I was 6 months old, and later ended their marriage in great anger. Through strife in our home, the enemy had stolen my family and threw us into a life of poverty, depression, anger, fear, and hopelessness.

My Mother was left broken, covered in rejection and anger, and had become physically ill from all the stress and depression she was facing. Dad was full of anger and left alone. Needless to say, our house was filled with oppression and broken hearts. I remember it feeling very "dark" all the time. The oppression I was under brought with it many nightmares and insecurities. Because of this, I was constantly being corrected in school for having a "bad attitude". This only heaped more condemnation upon me. It was like being punished for being a victim. And this happens every day, all over the world, to countless other victims.

During my childhood and most of my adult years, I was in desperate need of help and was in great need of a touch from heaven. Now I look back and see how the hand of the Lord protected us from complete destruction. It is clear to me that the enemy was working to destroy us completely.

BUT GOD HAS A PLAN!

The good news is that no matter what condition your family is in today, God has a plan to turn around every hopeless situation. He waits for us to turn our hearts toward Him, so He can work it all together for our good and His glory!

Ignorance concerning deliverance ministry and of the greatness of God's power kept me and my family in bondage. Jesus said, "then you will know the truth, and the truth will set you free." (John 8:32) Jesus is still our Deliverer, today!

**"For Zion's sake I will not keep silent,
for Jerusalem's sake I will not remain quiet,
till her righteousness shines out like the dawn,
her salvation like a blazing torch.
The nations will see your righteousness,
And all kings your glory;
You will be called by a new name
that the mouth of the Lord will bestow.
You will be a crown of splendor in the Lord's hand,
a royal diadem in the hand of your God.
No longer will they call you Deserted,**

**Or name your land Desolate,
But you will be called Hephzibah."
Isaiah 62:1-4**

Hephzibah means, "my delight is in her". Today, by His amazing grace, He desires to show His delight in you!

SONGS OF VICTORY

Today, He has given me a beautiful relationship with my husband, blessed, and anointed my children with His spirit, and filled my entire being with His perfect peace. Together, we are bringing the truth about Jesus that sets other captives free, to see other blind eyes opened, and to see others healed. May every wayward heart that reads this today, be turned back to the Heavenly Father that loves them, and know – He will do it for you, too! His word promises that He is no respecter of persons and NOTHING is impossible with God!

While I once saw God as an angry Father who was ready to condemn me for my horrible sin, He showed me His prodigal heart. He looked down the road waiting for me – looking for me to return. When I wandered too far and lost my way, He came looking for me. He loves us THAT much. When we turn and run to Him, and finally fall into His waiting arms, all He can think of is - how happy He is that we've come home into His arms of love. His next thought is to dress us with His clean, royal garments, and place His seal upon us, joyously marking us as His own.

He's the Father,
who longs for the whole world
to know His prodigal heart.

Turn to Him and run, today, with all of your heart. He's waiting with open arms. Then don't stop running until you are lost in Him. This is the secret to not only *The Mom Ministry,* but to true freedom, joy, for all of LIFE, and for all mankind...

It's eternal!

ten

Prayer That Moves Mountains,

FOR REAL!

"As for me, far be it from me that I should sin against the Lord by failing to pray for you…" I Samuel 12:23

 rayer is not a tiresome work we strive to accomplish in our own strength or desire. Prayer is simply coming into agreement with God's will with child-like faith. Agreeing with God's word allows the heavenly plans and Spirit of God to connect and be released in the earth. Each time we yield on bended knee, we

become an open piece of conduit for the Spirit of God to be poured into our homes and hearts. When the disciples asked Jesus to teach them to pray, Jesus responded with the Lord's prayer which included..."thy Kingdom come, thy will be done on earth as it is in heaven."

It's the place where our hearts meet and become one with His. It's the place where we exchange our love for one another. It's the place where His life is released into ours and we are enabled to abide in Him. Prayer is the place where we come to understand what our moment to moment purpose is.

Our altar of prayer can be either at our bedside, kneeling in our prayer closet, our bathroom, or a walk through the woods. It's where we are refreshed and strengthened, where we release all that weighs us down. Prayer is the place we are changed to be more like Jesus.

INTERCESSION THAT BREAKS THROUGH

**"He saw that there was
no one, he was appalled that there was
no one to intercede..."
Isaiah 59:16**

The Mom Ministry is one of intercession - not only prayers of blessing, but intercession that stands in the gap for our children's lives, sins, future, and ministries. It's prayer that establishes them in the Kingdom of God.

Intercession is prayer on behalf of someone else. The bible teaches that the righteous intercede before the Father for those who have fallen. As we intercede, we are reaching and meeting God seeking Him for His favor for another. Intercession is an act of selfless love and compassion.

In Genesis 18, Abraham interceded for Sodom. Moses interceded on behalf of the Hebrew people (Exodus 15). And, it's what Jesus is doing in this very moment for you and I. Therefore, we are each given a most priceless privilege and opportunity to partner with Christ by interceding for others. By doing so, we are literally stepping into His present work of the Kingdom with Him. What an awesome truth!

Intercessory prayer is not a calling for a select few in the body of Christ. The Bible teaches that intercession is a primary ministry of the entire church. Mark 11:17 says,

"...Is it not written: 'My house will be called a house of prayer for all nations?'

Each of our children has a heavenly purpose that God desires to break forth into the natural through our intercession. Even the child that is born through an unexpected or unplanned pregnancy holds within them gifts and eternal purpose from God to bless our lives and complete the plan of God for this generation. God's view is so much bigger than ours, His power so much greater than we can imagine.

The Mom Ministry provides us with an awesome privilege and responsibility. Each of our children are part of God's incredible and perfectly unfolding plan. They have a destiny that God desires to fulfill through them. Each has a heavenly purpose that will only break forth into the natural through intercessory prayer. You and I have an awesome opportunity and responsibility to be used by the Holy Spirit to birth this move of God through the coming generation.

"Before I formed you in the womb I knew *and* approved of you [as My chosen instrument], and before you were born I separated *and* set you apart, consecrating you; [and] I appointed you as a prophet to the nations."
Jeremiah 1:5 (Amplified)

The enemy is very aware of the danger to the kingdom of darkness when a Mother stands in the gap for her children and prays until something happens. Whether they are her maternal children, adopted or spiritual children, they need to be covered in our intercessory prayer. God wants to use us to cancel the plans the enemy has for our children. As we stand in the gap, petitioning God's throne of grace and mercy for them, the enemy is confronted with the God's Holy warring angels. This work we have before us, is of the war that began in the garden of Eden.

"And I will put enmity between you and the woman, and between your offspring and her Offspring: He will bruise and tread your head underfoot, and you will lie in wait and bruise His heel." Genesis 3:15(Amplified)

WARFARE PRAYER

"Misunderstanding the Enemy's Authority" –
The activity of Satan in the world is so obvious that many assume he has more authority and power than is

actually the case. **Others, of course, ignore or deny his existence and blame human beings or our environment for all the trouble.   Either of these extremes, as C. S. Lewis pointed out, is dangerous. And both positions leave us misunderstanding the enemy's authority and power.**[vi]

"What is Warfare Prayer," you may be asking? It's important for us to understand the power that we have in Christ, when we pray.   Our prayers are a deadly threat to the kingdom of darkness when we are clothed in the full armor of God, equipped with the sword of the Spirit (God's Holy Word), and wearing the mantle of authority we have been given through Christ Jesus.   The kingdom of darkness has schemed and worked feverishly since the Garden of Eden, to set up traps of worldliness, idolatry, and anything that will distract our children at a young age from following the One True God.   If we ignore our responsibility and privilege to pray, we're leaving our children wide open and unprotected from the enemy. God has called us to pray like never before.

Yes, the battle is the Lords. But this work in the spirit (that is done on our knees) is more real than World War II, Vietnam, Desert Storm, or the war against global terrorism.   This final war we are waging in the Spirit – is the war of all wars.   The battle has begun, and will continue until the end of this age. It's over the seed of faith in the hearts of our children and every soul that is to be a part of the fullness of the Harvest.   Satan does not want us to worship, serve, or fall in love with the One True God.

Each day we spend time sharing the truths of God's word with our children, it weakens the enemy's ability to draw them away from God. We can do so as we stroll down the sidewalk together, ride in the car to daycare, walk them to the school bus, or visit with them at the dinner table. Each moment is a priceless opportunity to plant an eternal seed of truth in their hearts and minds.

Filling our homes with the fragrance of prayer, draws the presence of the Holy Spirit, igniting the air with God's love and power. It invites the presence of the Lord that will convict our kids of sin, create a sense of safety and security in our homes, and nurture their deepest need for love. The Holy Spirit's presence in our homes will help inspire them to pursue the Christ for their purpose in life.

All of this serves as fertile ground – a safe haven, for our children to grow strong in their faith, until it is time to release them fully to fly.

WHAT KIND OF PRAYER

I have found two of the most powerful forms of prayer are that of praying in the spirit for my children, and praying the Word of God over their lives.

"In the same way, the Spirit helps us in our weakness. We do not know what we ought to pray, but the Spirit himself intercedes for us with groans that words cannot express. And he who searches our hearts knows the mind of the Spirit, because the Spirit intercedes for the saints in accordance with God's will." Romans 8:26, 27

The Holy Spirit helps us in our weakness when we don't know what we should pray.

"The earnest (heartfelt, continued) prayer

of a righteous man makes tremendous power
available [dynamic in its working]."
James 5:16 (Amplified)

Daily, the enemy will come against us with every distraction imaginable to hinder or stop us from praying. For he knows the tremendous power that God makes available to the humble soul who faithfully does so. We must resist every temptation with every ounce of strength we have. It has been said that those seated closest to Christ Jesus in heaven may not be the Pastors and Evangelists, preachers or deacons. But, the Grandma's and children who have done the mightiest work in the Kingdom of God – "the work of prayer".

It's not a chore, or part of our "To Do List". I call it a blessed right and privilege as a child of God and spiritual mother. It's our daily time of communion with the one who loves us most. The one who has all the answers, hope and strength I need for each day.

LORD, TEACH US TO PRAY

Not until I began to pray, "Lord, mold in me a prayer life like Jesus," did I truly see an extraordinary change in my prayer times. Before this point, I saw many precious times of victory in prayer. But after I began to pray this, I began to notice quiet changes, that weren't evident immediately. Then, over the course of time, I began to notice a greater peace and inner strength rising within.

We all have to start somewhere. God is looking at your heart and your willingness to yield to His plan for your family. Do you truly desire to draw closer to Him? To know Him more? To be intimate with Him?

Jesus Himself ministered out of a life of prayer. He knew the source of His strength came from His Father's throne each morning. Being fully God and fully Man, Jesus' ministry existed because of His intimate relationship with our Heavenly Father and the Holy Spirit. They moved together, as one, in unity and love. The fulfillment of His destiny and purpose was NOT possible apart from His deep, close, and very REAL relationship with them. And so it is for us.

The following is a brief description of six powerful elements of prayer that we use faithfully. God has used them to transform our family.

1. THE BLOOD OF JESUS

Each day, in prayer I apply the blood of Jesus over every one of my family members. It is one of the most valuable and powerful things that God has taught me in building and protecting my home and family.

"Now have come the salvation and the power and the kingdom of our God,
and the authority of his Christ.
For the accuser of the brothers,
who accuses them before our God day and night, has been hurled down.
They overcame him by the blood of the Lamb and the word of their testimony."
Revelation 12:10 – 11

As the enemy comes before our Father accusing our children and us, if we're not careful, we will begin to listen and agree with his lying thoughts that tell us that neither we, nor our children are good enough. We stand in the confidence and power of the blood of Jesus. In ourselves, none of us are worthy. But by the blood of the Lamb, we are washed and made pure. This is what enables us to come boldly before the throne of grace and receive mercy. Believing this truth in our hearts is what sets us free from perfectionism, performing, and "religion." What an amazing miracle - we are accepted just as we are, by the blood of the Lamb. This produces a change in our lives that can only come by receiving Jesus as the true giver of life and the redeemer of our souls! What an awesome truth to regularly remind our children of.

God's word says that satan is the father of lies and the truth is not in him. But the blood of Jesus, the shield of faith, and the word of our testimony are our defense and protection against condemnation, depression, sickness, and other attacks of the enemy. satan and all of his demons hate the blood of Jesus.

Daily, my husband and I take time to pray that the blood of Jesus will cover and protect our family, marriage, ministries, and all God has given us. Modeled after Leviticus 14:17, each day we ask God to place the blood covering:

- Over our ears, that we will listen ONLY to the voice of the Holy Spirit.
- Over our hands, that all of our work will be protected by His blood.
- And over our feet, that our path and ways will be protected from veering off the road of redemption, and keeping us on the straight and narrow. That our ministries and every place we put our feet to, will be protected from the plans of the enemy against us.

(Until my husband grew to the place that He wanted and sensed the need to join me, I used to do this on my own - God honored and blessed it). We have seen the powerful difference it has made in our lives for many years. It works, it's real, it's for today and it is necessary!

Remember this and teach your children: THE BLOOD OF JESUS protects and defends us. IT'S THE LINE SATAN WILL NOT CROSS.

I love to teach children that the blood of Jesus is the most powerful soap in all of creation. It's more powerful than bleach or bath soap. The perfect blood of Jesus blots out every sinful stain from our hearts and removes it forever.

> **"I, even I, am he who blots out your**
> **transgressions, for my own sake, and remembers**
> **your sins no more."**
> Isaiah 43:25

Moses instructed the Israelites to place the blood over the doorway of the their homes to protect them from the plague of the death angel who was to pass over.   Every household that did not apply it, was struck by this plague and judged by God.

> **"The blood will be a sign for you on the houses where**
> **you are; and when I see the blood, I will pass over you.**
> **No destructive plague will touch you**
> **when I strike Egypt."**
> Exodus 12:13

In the same way, it's only by the blood of Jesus that we can enter into a relationship with God our Father and escape the judgment for our sin. The same power exists to protect us from the enemy, today.

2. OUR AUTHORITY IN CHRIST

According to the Word of God, Jesus gave us HIS authority to use against the powers of darkness that work to stop the move of God in our family's lives. As we use the name of Jesus when we pray, the bible teaches us that all which God represents stands behind that name. Jesus finished His work on the cross, and just before ascending to heaven, gave us His authority. He then commissioned us to go and operate in His name, as His personal ambassadors.

He was serious about it! We must not shrink back from the work that He has given us. That work must begin on the home front. The enemy comes against our children to divide our household through strife, quarreling, envy, and sickness. As believers, we have been given the NAME ABOVE ALL NAMES to use against him. It's never too late to start.

John 15:1-17 is a clear picture given to us by Jesus. It shows the fruit of answered prayers that come when we abide in Him. An intimate relationship with Him is the basis for *The Mom Ministry* and victory in our homes. God is faithful – and takes care of his own.

3. PRAYERS OF AGREEMENT

"Again, I tell you that if two of you on earth agree about anything you ask for, it will be done for you by my Father in heaven. For where two or three come together in my name, there I am with them." Matthew 18:19, 20

"A house that is divided cannot stand". This is a strategy in every battle that the enemy knows very well. Strife and disagreement are two of the most common weapons he uses to come against our families. His goal is to destroy the family unit. He and his demons work daily to pit us against one another. Why does he do this? The enemy knows that if he is successful, we will not be unified and come together in prayers of agreement.   Ephesians 6 clearly shows us that it's not Mom and Dad battling, it's spirit versus spirit. It's not Rachel versus Amy, it's a spirit of strife and many times, our desire to demand our own way, that causes us to disagree. At all times we must remember it is "the enemy that is the enemy". Ephesians 6 teaches us that we battle not against flesh and blood, but against the powers and rulers in the spirit realm. It's spiritual warfare. But in Christ Jesus, we have the victory as we use the spiritual weapons He has given us.

Ephesians 6:13 – 18 is a great place to take kids and teach them about the full armor of God. Each morning you can practice "putting on the full armor of God," together. You may find it to be just as helpful for you as it is for them.

Using your imaginations, you can use your hands to motion that you are putting on the belt of truth, the breastplate of righteousness, readiness from the gospel of peace (on your feet), the shield of faith, the helmet of salvation, and the sword of the spirit. Then, you can pray that the Spirit of God will help you use them to stand your ground in the Spirit.

4. ABOVE ALL, LOVE ONE ANOTHER

When we minister in the Kingdom of God, all of it is to be done out of a heart filled with God's love. If our motive isn't love, it's doubtful that God is in the work. There's no greater weapon in spiritual warfare than God's unconditional love for one another. That's why the Bible commands us to love our enemies and do good to those who do not deserve it. Doing this defeats satan. But, the only place to get it, is in daily prayer or worship before the Lord. As we choose to be generous with love and mercy, it grows and spreads. It's the fastest diffuser of a disagreement in all of creation. We don't have to be "right", but we do need to be reconciled to God, and walk in love with one another.

Releasing love in the face of adversity, literally releases the Spirit of Almighty God into the situation. Devils run away screaming and defeated. Families reconcile, experience healing, and see healthy change, when God's LOVE is released.

When you find you can't do so, resist the enemy's tactics to divide you by making a decision to agree in prayer. Hold hands and begin to pray together, even if you're feelings are saying, "NO"! Remember, love is a decision to be selfless and to think of one another before our own selves, despite our feelings.

There's nothing that will make you love someone, like praying for them.

Your feelings will soon change, as you continue with a willingness to give your feelings to God, asking Him to change your heart and help you forgive. He will – EVERY TIME! You will find that your feelings will catch up, quickly.

5. THE NAME OF JESUS

The name of Jesus is above every name. The Bible says there is power in that name.

"And these signs will accompany those who believe: In my name they will drive out demons; they will speak in new tongues; they will pick up snakes with their hands; and when they drink deadly poison, it will not hurt them at all; they will place their hands on sick people, and they will get well." Mark 16:17, 18

When Jesus left this earth to go prepare a place for us, he left us with a great commission. That commission was not given with an expiration date. He expected the church to continue what He began until He returns for us. The Bible is clear that the last outpouring of the Holy Spirit will be greater than the former.

As believers, we are agreeing to partner with Him today to do that work in our homes and in the lives of our children. When we got saved, we received a full grown Jesus within us that is MORE than able to do exceedingly abundantly above and beyond what we can ask for or imagine (Ephesians 3:20). In the Book of Acts, the Holy Spirit baptized them to move in His power (see Acts 1:8), and so it is today. The power in the name of Jesus doesn't weaken with age. Hebrews 11:8 says, "Jesus Christ is the same yesterday, and today and forever." But there is a work that He is calling us to that is above and beyond our greatest imagination. It's the work of His Kingdom.

**John 6:29 says,
"The work of the Kingdom of God is this,**

to believe in the one that he has sent."

This is *The Mom Ministry.* To know God and to move in His spirit in such a way of love and grace that the unbelievers, broken, captive and hurting are drawn to know our Jesus.

Some years ago, before arriving at a training conference, I heard the Lord say something that sends chills down my spine each time I think of it. He said,

"Lisa, don't waste what I give you."

The Mom Ministry is a ministry of giving away all that He has given us. God is opening our eyes today to the reality that we are in the end time battle. Jesus is coming soon – it's a time to arise and pour out our lives like Jesus did. To not waste a drop of the truth and anointing we've been given and to fulfill the divine purpose for our lives. He's calling us to see our motherhood as a ministry to train our children to be in love with Jesus and fully believe His word. To encourage them to go and win their schools to Jesus, to lay hands on the sick in HIS NAME, and do all Jesus commanded us to do. The power we have in His name is still available to every believer today, and is to be used to make Jesus' love known to the world.

CHILDREN WHO MINISTER IN JESUS' LOVE AND POWER

While on a trip to Kampala, Uganda, last winter, we ministered to the children the truth of Jesus. They accepted Jesus into their lives and were healed, just like we read in the book of Acts. There is no greater miracle than receiving eternal life through Jesus. Seeing them healed in His name brought us great JOY! And something else happened that was also very thrilling.

The second day of one of our Children's Crusades, we asked all of the children who had been saved and healed to come forward and pray for the children that were in need of healing. We instructed them to do exactly what we did the day before. By faith, they laid their little hands on one another and in the name of Jesus prayed for healing for the others. In moments, we had more testimonies of miracles than we could record.

Tumors and lumps vanished from their bodies, malaria and fevers were healed, headaches, skin diseases, and countless others. The next day, a young girl who had never walked before was walking for the first time. Our mission is to teach them that after receiving Christ, inside of them is a full grown Jesus (just like adults have). And God desires to use them to do big things so that the earth can see His glory and goodness through each of them. Our children are part of God's plan to show the earth that He is the Lord.

Listen Mom, if you're truly serious about raising your kids to be operating in the power of God in a greater degree, I want you to hear something powerful the Lord said to me in March, 2002. I was in a precious time of worship, when the Holy Spirit began to speak to me:

"I will visit the children ~
We are going somewhere,"
the Lord said.

I then wept for the children
and for all those we have influence with.

"Lord," I responded, "if you don't touch and reveal
yourself to them, how will they ever have a chance
to be changed," I cried.
"Teach me your ways, Lord –
tell me what to do, so that I may be used to lead
them into your presence."

The Lord responded,

*"I will use the children
to confound the wise and the adults…
their mouths will drop open at the sight of my
visitation upon them."*

**We say, "Yes, Lord - - - - come visit and do ALL That
YOU PROMISED YOU WOULD DO.
Use our children to confound the wise, Father.
Teach me, O Lord, to walk in your ways and to
raise my children to know you like Samuel, like Moses,
like Peter and Paul, like Deborah and Esther.
Yes, Lord, do all that you please in and through our
children. Use us to bring glory to your Holy Name.
Father, I know the time is short, but I ask you to
redeem the time and forgive us
for the time we've wasted.
Restore all that we've lost, so that Jesus
will be given His rightful place in our home
and in the earth.
I ask this in the name that is above all names ~
The name of Jesus.   Amen.**

6. PRAYING THE WORD

Praying the word is an incredibly powerful way of aligning yourself and home with God's will.

Satan will do anything and everything possible to keep you from praying your children through. When you do, DIVINE power is released in the Spirit against the powers of darkness. Prayers of faith in God, releases power that MOVES MOUNTAINS. To hinder you, the devil will hurl every distraction at you that he possibly can. He knows when we get on our knees, it creates problems for him in the heavens. Angels go to battle for our children as we pray the Word of God over their lives. The Bible says the angels of God begin to go to work the moment they hear the voice of the word of God.

"Bless the Lord, ye his angels, that excel in strength, that do his commandments, hearkening unto the voice of his word."
Psalm 103:20 (KJV)

Angels listen for the voice of His word and move out to establish it in our lives. As we pray, we align ourselves with God's word, God's will, and God's weaponry, to bring His plans for our families into the earth.

As we pray, we are literally partnering with God Our Father, Jesus (the Chief Intercessor), the Holy Spirit who intercedes through us (Romans 8:26, 27), and the angels of God. It's undefeatable teamwork! And with God, we are in the majority! Who can stand against the Lord our God? He is our Loving, Almighty,

Omnipotent, All-Knowing, All-Seeing, and Supreme Lord.

TOGETHER, WE SAY, "YES, LORD"

There is nothing God can't do through a yielded vessel. God desires to use our ministries to our children to establish His will and Kingdom in the earth. But, He's calling us together, to arise and embrace it wholeheartedly. He's calling us to realize the urgency of the hour – and do what we know deep inside He's requiring of us. He's waiting for us to release Him fully into our homes, that the glory of the Lord will cover the earth as the waters cover the sea.

It's time to arise and let our light s shine, Moms ~ It's time to release the Spirit of Jesus…

Isaiah 60

**Arise, shine, for your light has come,
and the glory of the Lord rises upon you.
See, darkness covers the earth and thick
darkness is over the peoples,
but the Lord rises upon you
and his glory appears over you.
Nations will come to your light,
and kings to the brightness of your dawn.
Lift up your eyes and look about you;
all assemble and come to you;
your sons come from afar, and your daughters are
carried on the arm.**

Then you will look and be radiant,
your heart will throb and swell with joy;
the wealth on the seas will be brought to you,
to you the riches of the nations will come.
Who are these that fly along like clouds,
like doves to their nests?
Surely the islands look to me;
in the lead are the ships of Tarshish,
bringing your sons from afar,
with their silver and gold,
to the honor of the Lord your God,
the Holy One of Israel,
for he has endowed you with splendor...
The glory of Lebanon will come to you,
the pine, the fir and the cypress together, to adorn the
place of my sanctuary;
and I will glorify the place of my feet. The sons of your
oppressors will come bowing before you;
all who despise you will bow down at your feet
and will call you The City of the Lord,
Zion of the Holy One of Israel...
Although you have been forsaken and hated,
with no one traveling through, I will make you the
everlasting pride and the joy of all generations.
You will drink the milk of nations and be nursed at royal
breasts.
Then you will know that I, the Lord, am your Savior, your
Redeemer, the Mighty One of Jacob.
Instead of bronze I will bring you gold, and silver in
place of iron. Instead of wood I will bring you bronze,
and iron in place of stones. I will make peace your
governor and righteousness your ruler. No longer will
violence be heard in your land, nor ruin or destruction
within your borders,
But you will call your walls Salvation

and your gates Praise.
The sun will no more be your light by day,
nor will the brightness of the moon shine on you,
for the Lord will be your everlasting light, and your God
will be your glory.
Your sun will never set again, and your moon will wane
no more;
The Lord will be your everlasting light, and your days of
sorrow will end. Then will all your people be righteous
and they will possess the land forever. They are the
shoot I have planted, the work of my hands, for the
display of my splendor. The least of you will become a
thousand, the smallest a mighty nation.
I am the Lord;
In it's time I will do this swiftly."

(Isaiah 60:1-5, 8-9, 13-22)

eleven

The Arsenal

"I've made you an Arsenal," the Lord whispered to me.

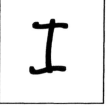 nside every one of us is a spiritual storehouse. God desires to fill us with His strength and divine weapons of warfare to stand victoriously in our faith (Psalm 18:30-36). It's literally impossible to live a life of peace and righteousness outside of learning how to use the spiritual weapons that God has given us.

Our job is to believe and obey God's word, no matter what it looks like. Our mind is truly the battlefield. One of our priorities is to train up our children to live victoriously in the character and love of Christ Jesus.

I felt it was critical that I take at least a small portion of pages and dedicate it to some of the most revolutionary lessons I've learned. In the early days, getting the basics under my belt enabled me to be jumpstarted and not walk in as much defeat in my mind and emotions. I praise the Lord for revealing these powerful truths to me. Until I learned these lessons, I struggled greatly in my walk with the Lord.

You'll find in this chapter some primary areas that the enemy likes to target our families with. I've outlined some powerful ways God has given us to stand against him. Doing so, frees us to enjoy the Lord and His presence in our homes more. When we begin to walk in the truths of the Word more readily, a shift takes place in our spiritual journey. We shift from walking in the "defensive" with the enemy to the "offensive". When this happens, he is no longer in our face, but under our feet, and we find ourselves walking in victory.

Today, we want to work on building up the walls around our homes and children. We need a hedge of protection and a foundation built upon prayer and the Word of God. This helps to keep our hearts, minds, and homes free of hindrances.

VICTORY OVER FEAR

After we are saved, we are not initially as much of a threat to the enemy and His kingdom, until we begin to open our mouths and speak the truth.

**Revelation 12:11 says,
"They overcame him by the blood of the lamb,
and by the word of their testimony;"**

Sharing what God has done for us, living God's Word, and praying that the blood of Jesus will cover us, defeats the enemy. You are not a threat to the enemy unless you walk in obedience. FEAR is a lie – designed to stop you, distract you, or hinder you from doing what God wants you to. Fear is the opposite of faith. Hebrews 11:1 tells us that:

"Now faith is being sure of what we hope for and certain of what we do not see."

Fear is having faith that the negative is greater than God's word. It's a smokescreen and can only be defeated by moving forward in obedience to God's word and direction. As you step through the smokescreen (wall of fear), God gives you the victory and you are then able to see, "it really WAS just a lie". The enemy uses the lies of fear to try to deceive us that we are not able to do what God has told us to.

Fear comes in all shapes and sizes. Fear of man, fear our children will not come to Christ, fear that they will make poor choices, fear that we are not doing enough, fear of failing, fear of being wrong, fear of losing, fear of succeeding, fear of being noticed or looked at, fear of being embarrassed, fear of the dark, fear of being scolded, fear of being misunderstood, fear of being hurt, fear of losing something valuable to us, and countless others.

I'm sure you can add some others to the list, as well. The good news is,

"I can do everything through Him who
gives me strength." Philippians 4:13

But how do we break free into greater levels of
courage and faith? Fear is listed in the Strong's
Concordance over 300 times in the Old and New
Testaments. God knows we are human and struggle
with fear, but commands us countless times in scripture
to "fear not". One of my favorite passages of scripture
is Psalm 34:4. It says,

**"I sought the Lord, and He answered me;
he delivered me from all my fears."
Psalm 34:4**

Many times fear comes to stop us from obeying
God the instant the Lord tells you to do something.
Every time we obey God it is detrimental to the
Kingdom of Darkness. The Lord spoke to me one day
concerning this while facing incredible opposition from
the enemy to obey God by stepping out in faith.

The Lord said,

"Your obedience releases My power."

Counter the lies of fear with the truth, the sword
of the Spirit, and OBEDIENCE! To build up your faith to
do so, list some of your favorite scriptures concerning
fear on a small sheet of paper, even laminate it if you
like. Keep them in your purse or bible, and begin to
boldly and audibly quote them every day, until your
feelings begin to change. Remember faith is not a
feeling, and faith comes by hearing the Word of God!

Pray and seek the Lord. Drawing close to Him, and focusing on how great and mighty God is, causes us to be lifted above the smokescreen so that we can see the circumstances from God's standpoint. Ask the Lord to deliver you from fear, and begin to praise Him for His grace and mighty power. The enemy will weaken by doing so – and absolutely run away trembling as you praise the Name of Jesus.

And no matter what - if the emotion of fear or nervousness doesn't go away, Obey God anyway!

Do so until your feelings line up with God's word and you have the victory. Each time you do, you will break into greater levels of freedom and confidence in the Name of the Lord.

Fasting and prayer is also a powerful weapon against the enemy. The Lord had me fast and pray for a month to break free from the fear of speaking in front of people. This particular fear I was facing was more than butterflies and sweaty palms, it was paralyzing. I was so afraid, it almost immobilized me. But in order to teach and preach the Word of God, I needed to break through that fear wall. The war in my mind seemed to be the greatest until I would stand up and open my mouth. Each time I did, I gained strength in the Spirit and victory over the war in my mind. Hallelujah – the weapons God has given us in the spirit are MIGHTY IN GOD to tear down every stronghold! (II Corinthians 10:4).

I find that praying in the Spirit strengthens me beyond comprehension. As I do, my inner man is strengthened and I walk in a stronger sense of faith and victory than ever before. Every day I learn more how to walk in all that Jesus paid for. Romans 8:26 and 27 teach us that the Spirit knows our weaknesses and prays through us, what is in accordance with the will of God. He is indeed our helper in every area of need.

Today I'd like to share a few truths that God used to open my eyes to ways that the enemy was getting in and robbing me of the promises and inheritance that Jesus paid for me to have. I believe as you read, pray, listen, and study these passages for yourself, you too will discover the path to greater freedom and victory in Jesus.

VICTORY OVER DOUBT

"If any of you lacks wisdom, he should ask God, who gives generously to all without finding fault, and it will be given to him.
But when he asks,
he must BELIEVE and NOT DOUBT,
because he who doubts is like a wave of the sea, blown and tossed by the wind.
That man should not think he will receive anything from the Lord; he is a double-minded man, unstable in all he does.
James 1:5-7

Sitting at my kitchen table one day in prayer, I asked, "Lord, how do you BELIEVE and NOT DOUBT"?

When believing God for something miraculous, how do you walk in a level of faith without doubting? How do you stop the thoughts from bombarding your mind when the doctor calls and tells you your test results are abnormal? This question plagued me for years after our second miscarriage (early in our marriage). We did all we knew the Bible taught us, in order to receive healing, but I was still overcome by doubt every day that I prayed. The problem was not in God's Word, it was that I needed to gain more understanding on how to overcome doubt!   I continued to struggle greatly in my walk with the Lord until He taught me a valuable truth.

God did indeed give me the answer to my question that afternoon when I asked Him to tell me how to BELIEVE and NOT DOUBT.

Deep inside I heard that "still small voice" whisper,

"doubt is a fiery dart from the enemy designed to knock holes in your faith".

Upon hearing this, I realized something powerful that forever changed me, "doubt was a *thought* from the enemy – therefore I can RESIST or reject it, just like any other lie he tries to tell me."   I began to realize, that in the same way that the enemy lies to get me to not obey the Lord, I could say, "NO" just as easily and not buy into the lie he was trying to sell me.   I realized for the first time in my life, the only things I can control are the thermostat, and the thoughts that I allow to linger in my mind. I can't control always the thoughts coming in, but I can control which ones I allow to stay and grow.

God taught me to begin to sift through each one as it comes in, checking to see if it matches God's word, and if not, I realized I could reject it immediately before it had a chance to take root and grow.

Is it sin to doubt? Continually giving into doubt, causes us to forfeit the blessings that we receive by faith that God will answer our prayers. It's another way the enemy has of stealing, killing, or destroying the awesome things that God has to give us. My antidote came when I began to recognize the doubt and counter it by praying, "Lord, help me overcome every doubting thought from the enemy." He is waiting and willing to help if we'll only ask.

Why is it important to not allow doubt to take root in my mind? Because Jesus said, "the work of God is this: to believe in the one that He sent" (John 6:29). It takes faith to obey and activate the power of God in our lives. If faith catapults us forward, doubt throws us back. The enemy knows the great damage we can God's charge against Israel for ignoring His law and not clinging to the knowledge of His word was this,

"...my people are destroyed for lack of knowledge. Because you have rejected knowledge, I also reject you as my priests; because you have ignored the law of your God, I also will ignore your children."
Hosea 4:6

On the flip side of this passage, we can see that by honoring the word of God and *not* rejecting or refusing to gain Godly knowledge, we will gain priceless treasures. By honoring the word of God, we will not be destroyed, but restored, and our children will NOT be ignored, but attended to by our Father.

My struggles with doubt didn't begin with my needing a miracle of healing for my babies. Doubt seemed to attack me every time I prayed for something. I would become discouraged and then give up. The enemy was able to steal my ability to believe through deception. Needless to say, for most of my life, I had a very hard time receiving answers to my prayers. This kept me walking in a lot of fear which for many years compelled me to be an extremely controlling person. Because of all the fears I had, I felt that I needed to control everything and everyone to keep myself safe from getting hurt or rejected.

Now you can see more, how doubt, fear, and control work together – to attack our faith. Doubt causes a chain reaction that works to keep us locked outside of a life lived in faith and victory.

When Jesus set me free, I found myself free to have many friendships and relationships that were not possible beforehand. I found myself able to reach out to people I did not know without fearing that I would be rejected or disliked. I was free to be able to show the love for people that I've always had. The Bible says, "perfect love casts out all fear."

Here is another powerful weapon of the Word to add to your arsenal:

"The weapons we fight with are not the weapons of the world. On the contrary, they have divine power to demolish strongholds. We demolish arguments and every pretension that sets itself up against the knowledge of God, and we take captive every thought to make it obedient to Christ". II Corinthians 10:5

The Bible says, "divine power" is contained in the weapons we fight with. God's power is far beyond anything earthly. This scripture is what the Lord used to teach me how to sift through each in-coming thought. In the same way I am responsible for keeping my heart and home clean, I am responsible for guarding my thoughts and keeping them clean. Our life goes in the direction of our most dominant thought. Allowing ourselves to entertain every in-coming thought is as dangerous as leaving your front and back door open while wild wolves are running around in your yard. They will run in the door, take over, ransack you and leave you hurting and bleeding in the corner (if you survive). Guard them! You and your family will be blessed for it!

WRITE THEM DOWN

Prayer has changed our home. Here's another way, the Lord intervened to transform our marriage into a place of safety and blessing. For more than the first half of our marriage, I was plagued with being sharply angered at my husband for no apparent reason. I was left feeling condemned after every encounter. He was left badgered and confused. I had prayed about it and asked the Lord to change me and help me be a loving wife with sweet words, but I just didn't seem to be changing.

God had led us through many trials and fires, keeping us together, working on one thing at a time in our marriage. He worked on our finances, then our parenting skills, then the time came for Him to work on our marriage. Good thing He doesn't do the work to change us all at once, we wouldn't be able to survive the pressure of the molding process.

I remember that my mood would be fine and pleasant until right before He'd arrive home from work. It seemed that He'd walk in the door, and my feelings would instantly change towards him. Or, I'd be walking through the house, carrying clothes in from the laundry room, and suddenly a surge of anger would rise up in me.

One day, the Lord whispered to me, "write down your thoughts". What a strange thing to tell me to do. But, I sensed as usual, that He was telling me to do so for a good reason, so I obeyed.

I began to record every thought that would come to my mind concerning my husband starting 10 minutes before He was due home. Before I tell you about the amazing thing that happened, I'd like to share the list of thoughts I had that day, it went something like this:

Ten minutes before he arrived home one day I recorded my thoughts as follows:

"Oh good, Andy's coming home soon."
"The boys will be happy."
"Dinner – oh no, not enough eggs to make the frosting for dessert."
"Maybe Andy can run out and grab some."
"Last time he took so long, though."
"Time's too short, by the time he does that, dinner will be getting cold."
"Hope he's not late again."
"I remember the last time, it took almost an hour"
"Slow – he's always so slow. (I felt tension arise in me)"
"Why didn't I just put it on my shopping list the other day? (more tension)"
"Where is he? He's late again..." (Anger starts)
"Why can't I count on him to be here on time?"
"He doesn't care." (More anger, discouragement)
"I'm left to handle all the pressure, again. (exaggeration and more anger)"
"He always leaves me to fix everything. (not true)."

Just then, Andy walked in the door, "Hi honey, how are you, " he said?
(I turned around and gave him my back (Angry).

Andy's thinking, "Thanks a lot honey, you really know how to make me feel cared about, don't you?" Andy thought to himself, "What is HER problem? Nice welcome home THIS is!"

WOE! In a few minutes, my thoughts escalated from "Good, Andy's coming home," to anger – and "He doesn't care about me." This equals a possible argument and a home that is filled with tension and strife!

God in his wisdom prompted me to write my thoughts for an eye opening reason. He was opening my eyes to the importance of guarding my thoughts. Until that day, I truly didn't realize that the enemy was feeding me all of these suggestions that Andy didn't care. My feelings simply followed the suggestions the enemy was feeding me.

He was exaggerating and telling me lies that Andy was ALWAYS late (not true), and using them to fill my heart with tension and strife towards my husband. The enemy's plan is to divide and conquer our homes. If our thoughts aren't guarded, he will succeed.

From that day forward I realized that if the thought wasn't true, honest, just, pure, of good report, then it wasn't for me to be thinking about…

Philippians 4:8
"Finally, brothers, whatever is true, whatever is noble, whatever is right, whatever is pure, whatever is lovely, whatever is admirable – if anything is excellent or praiseworthy – THINK ABOUT SUCH THINGS."

By giving me that instruction, God was opening my eyes to what the enemy was doing to my family and I. God was beginning to establish this scripture in my life and home. He was giving me more building blocks to build my home with. This is another valuable truth to teach our children as they grow. Every thought that enters our mind is not true! We must make sure they line up with the truth (God's Holy Word), before we accept them and live by them.

God was expecting me to be the gatekeeper of my thoughts toward every person and situation I came in contact with (starting with my husband and children). I am to sift through and reject the thoughts that lead me to anger and resentment towards others, and nurture the ones that promote love, peace, contentment and harmony.

When I sat down and showed Andy the record of thoughts from that day, and shared with him how I had been praying for God to help me be a sweeter more pleasant wife, we both hugged and thanked the Lord. We were so grateful to Him for providing the key of wisdom which unlocked us from a very destructive cycle in our home.

That day, I would say that about 90% of our arguments and quarrels were removed from our marriage with that one simple direction from the Lord. The Holy Spirit saved us about 3 years of marriage counseling with that one simple directive. How I love the Lord for being so good to us! It's true – the Holy Spirit is our Counselor! God wants your marriage and relationships with your children and family to be filled with His love and harmony! And it's possible – if you just ask, believe, and are willing to adjust yourself to line up with His word.

Are you having difficulty in a certain area, too? Maybe it's your teenager or child, or your husband, sister, or employer. I encourage you to take 5 minutes around the time of the reoccurring incident and record your thoughts. Then ask the Holy Spirit to help you see where the problem is so that it can be corrected. Take Philippians 4:8 and apply it immediately and watch the enemy lose his grip.

THOMAS, THE DOUBTER

In John, Chapter 20, the Bible says that the Apostle Thomas doubted Christ's resurrection. This proves that though we are human and walk closely with Jesus, our natural man struggles to look with our eyes, and be able to believe fully in God's power. Jesus' response was merciful and correcting. He asked Thomas to place his finger in the wounds in His hands and side, and then told him to, "stop doubting and believe". Then Jesus followed with some powerful words,

"Because you have seen me, you have believed; blessed are those who have not seen and yet have believed. Jesus did many other miraculous signs in the presence of his disciples, which are not recorded in this book. But these are written that you may believe that Jesus is the Christ, the Son of God, and that by believing you may have life in his name."
John 20:29-31

"Believing" brings the blessing of God! By resisting the enemy and submitting to God, the enemy must flee. As Jesus Himself defeated the enemy in the wilderness, we must also defeat the enemy by being filled with the Spirit, quoting scripture, and praying that the grace of God will abound and help us in our areas of weakness. Building ourselves up in the Word and in the Spirit keeps us strong and able to move forward in our growth of faith. Every trial and test increases our faith to believe God more and more! Remember the Holy Spirit is our helper and teacher.

VICTORY OVER UNBELIEF

Like doubt, unbelief traps us in a place of inability to receive all that God has for us. However to the believer, "everything is possible for him...," Mark 9:23.

Early on, I had been wrestling with some things that a leader in my church had been saying. The more he spoke, the more confused I became. I felt troubled in my spirit and once again took my dilemma to prayer. The Lord is so faithful to answer us when we ask. He wants us to understand and know Him and His ways.

My answer came in the form of a dream I had later that night. I had dreamt there was a long line of church people standing in a row. Each of them had a wolf mask on. In the dream, I walked up to each person and put my hand on their forehead and said, "in the Name of Jesus..." I continued to do this, but grew more and more confused when I saw that there were layers of masks that each one had been wearing. When I awakened I was troubled and decided to ask the Lord about it in prayer. The Lord's response was simply this, "The wolf has come to confuse you, target the unbelief with the sword of the Spirit." Immediately after I heard those words, a rush of peace blew through my heart and mind, leaving me feeling relaxed and at ease again.

God is faithful and the sword of the Spirit is living and active, sharper than a two edged sword. After this encounter with the Lord, I understood more how powerful and effective He is to keep us walking in truth and clarity. How good the Holy Spirit is to guide us into all truth, to lead us in the way we should go. He is our teacher, helper, and counselor.

Scripture does not tell us to be fearful in the sense of being afraid of the dark, but instead, to have a holy fear that we cannot take our faith and walk with the Lord for granted. We are to be conscious of where we are in our journey. The Bible teaches that unbelief is a serious spiritual problem that can lead to our being cut off from the rest of the vine or branch (Romans 11:20). Not believing God for a healing miracle may not send us to hell, but not believing that the blood of Jesus is the only way to be made righteous before God, can!

Clearly, unbelief is a serious spiritual condition of the heart that can be overcome by using the sword of the spirit. Unbelief closes a door, making us unreceptive and hardened against hearing the voice of God. It can be viewed in a sense, as a 'wall'. Unbelief causes us to resist the Holy Spirit and directly works against faith. The Word of God is anointed with spiritual power that acts as a battering ram, breaking through those walls. Repeatedly quoting, praying, and studying scripture – breaks it down, blow by blow. Leaving our mind renewed and faith strengthened.

In our children, especially teens that have had ample time for the enemy to construct walls of unbelief around their hearts, your best strategy is to pray the word, using scriptures that the Holy Spirit continually brings to your mind. Never underestimate the tremendous power in the Word of God and in the Spirit as you pray. These are mighty to tear down strongholds. As you pray, release your faith, believing wholeheartedly that God will reward you for diligently seeking Him.

You will sense a powerful change in the atmosphere in your home, faith will continue to grow in your own heart, the enemy's grip will loosen, and over time, you will see the Holy Spirit soften their hearts and make it harder and harder for them to say, "no" to Him.

TEACHING OUR CHILDREN

As we grow in faith in these areas, we must be teaching our children, and imparting into their lives, all God has given us. The Bible teaches us to share these great things that God has done for us with them, making the most of every opportunity. It equips them with the spiritual weapons and armor they need to stand against the enemy in their schools, on the playground, against nightmares, etc. Yes, God wants to use them everywhere they go, also!

Deuteronomy, Chapter 11 teaches us that our children have not seen all that God has done in our lives (the miracles, the times of great growth and victory). So often we forget to share these experiences with our children, thinking they might not understand or be able to receive spiritual things. However, verse 7 says,

**"But it was your own eyes that saw all these
great things the Lord has done...
Fix these words of mine in your hearts and minds;
tie them as symbols on your hands
and bind them on your foreheads.
Teach them to your children, talking about them**

**when you sit at home and when you walk along
the road, when you lie down and when you get
up. Write them on the doorframes of your houses
and on your gates, so that your days
and the days of your children
may be many in the land..."
Deuteronomy 11:7, 18-21**

Our children are spiritual sponges. As you share spiritual truths with them, the Holy Spirit will plant seeds of faith and wisdom in their hearts, and help them see how much Moms and Dads need to depend upon God, also. It's another way of building your home up in the spirit and in wisdom, erecting walls of faith and truth that helps to keep the enemy out. It's part of preparing them for their work in the Kingdom.

MAKING YOUR HOME A PLACE OF PURITY AND REFUGE

On our front door post, we've mounted a medal plate inscribed with Joshua 24:15,

**"As for me and my house,
we will serve the Lord."**

Scripture is mounted on different places on our walls and refrigerator. Each one sows a powerful seed and memory in the hearts and minds of our boys. They live in a refuge surrounded by solid unbreakable walls of the Word of God, blessing, and faith. As I walk through the house and pray each day, I invite the Holy

Spirit to fill each room with His peace, love, faith, joy, and contentment. I pray that His presence will fill our home and that warring angels will be stationed at every doorway.

As the Spirit leads me to, I use anointing oil to anoint the doorways, beds, pillows, chairs and furniture, in our home. Setting all of them apart for holy use. Asking the Lord to fill each place with His presence, ensuring our home is clean of all fear, division, strife, sickness, etc.

As I pray, I remain open to the Holy Spirit's leading and ask Him to reveal any thing that may be a spiritual danger to our family or children. Such as Harry Potter trading cards or paraphernalia, new age paraphernalia, pornography, books on magic from the school library or horror movies that may have been borrowed from friends at school. The Holy Spirit will reveal anything that should not be there.

Each of these things, gives the enemy a right to enter your home and inflict you and your family with some or all of the following: nightmares, panic attacks, sickness, strife, confusion, deception, demonic visitations, witchcraft, etc.

See the recommended book list in the back for further study on this subject.

Over the years, learning these things has helped our lifestyle and home change to be a place of peace, harmony, faith, healing, and deliverance. Our home is now a place that the Lord blesses with His presence, daily. Our desire is to make our home a place for the Lord's presence to feel welcome, honored, and comfortable in. We have adjusted our home life to revolve around Him, so that He is given the first and highest place of honor.

WORSHIP, THEN WORK

One of the best ways I know to keep the enemy under our feet is to understand the importance and necessity of daily worship. Mom's who minister, worship ~ then work. My heart is filled with hope and strength, each time I think of it – for God didn't call us to be a shining replica of today's modern "Super-Mom". Dashing at the speed of light from event to event, exhausting ourselves as the "World's Busiest Mom". He called us to be obedient to His word and His will, and make time to daily sit at His feet, as Mary did. Martha concerned herself too much with all the things that had to be done.

Following Mary's example, leads me to Jesus' grace and anointing. I then have an overflow of His presence to do the rest of my day's work. God's priorities are to be our priorities, not the other way around. When our children are tiny and in diapers, just "keeping up" with all the daily responsibilities is a great challenge. But God is faithful to us! I found that God's grace was more than enough to meet my inability to spend as much time in prayer and worship as I wanted to. Though I had less minutes in His presence, His grace saw my willing heart and made up the difference (in time). God made sure that our time together was "as potent" as it was before. God understands and sees our hearts and willingness to meet with Him.

Even so, we must be careful to stay balanced and not eliminate our daily time with Him. Equally, we must guard against letting things of the world, crowd out our precious time with Him. There's no other way to continue abiding in Him. Our priorities must be God first, then family, then our work.

In Luke 10:38-41, Mary was the worshipper, while Martha was busy about the many responsibilities of the day. There's a timely and life-changing message in this passage of scripture for today's Moms. It's for those who have ears to hear it, and the wisdom to put it into action. As busy as Jesus life was, He understood the necessity and blessing of withdrawing into His Father's presence, daily. It was His number one priority. He set this example for us to follow.

The Mom Ministry is released through hearts that know the priceless treasure and secret of faithfully sitting at the feet of Jesus. Then, and only then, are we spiritually ready to minister and do the work of the Kingdom in our home and outside it's walls.

The more we worship Him, the more His love frees us to love others!

This is the source of our daily strength and peace. By so doing, we walk from a 'resting position' relying upon His power daily in our lives to do the changing. A heart that worships the Lord daily has no room in it for stress or anxiousness. It's filled with the fruit of His Spirit.

This is the secret of life in the Spirit that Romans Chapter 8 speaks of. As we trust in His grace and power to do the work through us, we're free to enjoy our life in Christ and our families.

We can't wait until Sunday to worship! From your heart, you can worship Him while you: work, drive, walk, sing, relax in a chair, standing, kneel, or sit. Anywhere we are becomes a sanctuary, the moment you focus your heart and mind upon Him and tell Him of His goodness and beauty in your life. If possible, you can purchase a worship album from your local Christian store and worship as you wash dishes, or in the car (on the way to a meeting). You can play it softly in the background as you pray and read the Word. You may find it is easier sometimes to "enter into His presence" as you begin to move into a lifestyle of worship. And this is only the beginning. There are depths in God that lead us beyond the veil, where we experience the fullness of His glory. It's the Holy of Holies.

When the clouds of depression, PMS, or frustration begin to move in – play a Praise and Worship tape or CD and begin to praise and worship Jesus (in the midst of it). Watch the "SONshine" break forth and blow away the clouds of darkness. God wants us to worship ad pray until we pass the place of repentance and forgiveness; pass the place of waiting in His presence, until our heart is broken and softened, to receive another day's in-filling of His spirit. All of creation was made to worship Him in spirit and in truth. These are the worshippers that God seeks. He's calling us today to worship until we see His face. For the hungering heart, there is always MORE of Him...

My Christian walk was dramatically changed when I added daily praise and worship to my time with the Lord! I have learned the importance of balancing the Word, Prayer, and Worship, each day.

Not enough Worship – we SHRIVEL UP
Not enough Word – we DRY UP
Not enough Prayer – we BLOW UP

When we fail miserably by an out of balance schedule or by letting worry, fear, or selfishness creep in, we need to fall to our knees and seek His mercy and grace, again! The Bible tells us that the blood of Jesus is available to us every day, for every sin. But we must take the time to confess it, to pray, and to turn from our sin, so that we can be cleansed. Then, we are ready to worship Him and continue until we are in the throne room, in the spirit. Each time, He restores our hurting heart, strengthens us, revives us, and empowers us. This brings God joy and glory, and positions us to be his anointed vessels, so that He can release His power and love through us.

Why did I include the topic of "worship" as one of our weapons in our spiritual arsenal? Because it not only blesses the Lord and lifts us high above the circumstances, it's a powerful weapon to drive the enemy away. The devil hates when we worship the Lord. It drives him away screaming, covering his ears. The Bible says that God inhabits the praises of His people. And where there is some serious praise and worship happening, the enemy does NOT like to be. Our worship, defeats the enemy and invites the presence of the Lord.

Next time you find yourself discouraged, down in the dumps, worried, or feeling under the weather...check your arsenal and pull out some of your best worship and praise choruses...sing them with your whole heart, finding everything you can to thank the Lord for in your life...and watch the dark clouds blow away in moments.

God loves to hear His children sing Him songs. In return, He blesses us with His sweet and mighty presence ~ He is more than able to take care of our enemies for us, leaving us free and uplifted to enjoy our life with our families.

twelve

Advanced Mom Ministry

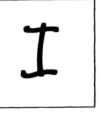n the Spring of the year 2000, just before awakening, I heard the voice of the Lord say,

"[You] are part of the Restorational Movement."

He wasn't referring to me only, but I knew that (You) was referring to all those I am "connected" with in the spirit. When the Lord began to reveal to my husband

and I that He was restoring His Church to once again be like the Book of Acts, He began to open up a whole world of understanding which we had not previously been aware of. We had never heard such things in church before the Lord began to speak this to our hearts.

We began searching for churches that were like the Lord had spoken to us about. The only thing that came close were the ones that we heard were being impacted by Holy Spirit revivals. Though we found many good churches, we were looking for one that had all the qualities we found in the Book of Acts.

We came across people here and there that were scattered and were also looking for the same things. Once and awhile, we would drive great distances to find that the only thing that looked like the Acts Church was the sign on the building. Desperate for more of God, we began to worship using CD's in our house and invite friends that we found that were also hungering for more of Him. God began to answer our prayers of faith and heal broken hearts, relationships, back injuries, fevers, flu symptoms, cancer, headaches, skin rashes, migraine headaches, the list goes on and on.

But it didn't stop there. We began to have dreams and visions, experience healing and miracles almost on a daily basis. What is so amazing, is our children began to have these experiences, too. Andrew, at the age of 5 began to pray as the Spirit led him to. You could tell that these prayers were not coming from him, but from the Holy Spirit. He would tell us that when he grows up he is going to be a Pastor who lays hands on the sick in wheelchairs and see them healed. AJ as tiny as he was began to wake up in the night and have visions and preach to us about Jesus.

A CLASSROOM EXPERIENCE WITH THE LORD

Little did we know, the Acts Church experience had fallen on the ordinary people in OUR OWN HOUSEHOLD and family! As we began to share what God was doing in our home, people began to get saved and the phone began to ring with calls for prayer. Young couples from all different denominational backgrounds began to show up at our door with tears in their eyes saying they wanted what we have in their own lives. We first made it clear to them, that it wasn't "us" at all, that it was the Holy Spirit at work in our lives. All we were doing was pursuing God with all of our hearts and minds, while obeying every little thing the Holy Spirit told us to do.

GET READY ~ JESUS IS GONNA' TURN YOUR WORLD UPSIDE DOWN

As we continued to travel this most exciting road, the Lord made it clear and confirmed again and again, that "the church" we see today is in the *process* of being restored by His spirit to be like the Book of Acts (except with a greater outpouring). He is moving by His Spirit to restore the body of Christ to a place of unprecedented unity, love, and faith. His church is a church that walks in His great love with miracles, signs, and wonders following. Looking back we remembered that He said, "My church WILL BE the Book of Acts, again".

This "Acts" experience happens through ordinary people who are hungry for more of God and will pursue Him with all their heart, no matter how old or young we might be. Except, this is on a much larger scale and with greater fervency than the world has ever seen before!

Our burden to see the Body of Christ unify increased with every passing day. Our hearts were stirred to intercede and cry out for the lost to be saved, for the Body of Christ as a whole to be purified, reconciled, unified, and restored. And God began to open our eyes to the reality that this move of God includes the children in a great and mighty way!

God revolutionized our lives and the way we saw and functioned as "the church". We began to see that it is beyond denominational, racial, and ethnic circles. It is God's Word and His Spirit doing something bigger and more alive than our minds can begin to grasp.

From housewives, plumbers, businessmen, children, farmers, and teens, to grocery clerks, women and grandparents, God is waking up His body to realize, "IT'S TIME". The Lord put in our hearts that there isn't a place, a town, or a business that will not be impacted and touched by this massive end-time move of His Spirit. It's so big (and unfolding so perfectly and rapidly), that the devil and all of his hordes can't even begin to keep up with it! Who is like OUR GOD ?!

With every passing day, we are urged by the Holy Spirit that THIS is the day of salvation and outpouring. Time is shorter than ever before. He began to show us how much of what has been lost in today's modern day church is in need of being restored to the Body of Christ. And He's doing it in the hearts of each of those who are tuning in to listen and follow Him without compromise. God is moving by His

Spirit in the hearts and minds of people all over the world to do that. They are waking up to the reality that the Acts church is for today. We need it in order to live the abundant life Christ paid for, so that the fullness of the harvest can come in. TODAY IS YOUR DAY, Mom! IT'S TIME for your family...it's time for your children. God placed you there because He wants to do something mighty through you. (See Acts 17:26 and 27.)

KIDS AND TEENS ARE PART OF GOD'S PLAN, TOO!

God is doing something extraordinary in and through the young people today. God is giving them a burden to intercede for the lost, to worship and seek to know the very REAL and living God. They don't care if it costs them everything ~ they're hungering instead for EVERYTHING they can find IN HIM! They are discovering how FUN God is! God is using kids today that are hungering for more of Him. They too are a vital part of the body of Christ and are in great need of preparation for what's ahead. We are needed to prepare them.

RAISING FIVE-FOLD MINISTERS

Ephesians, Chapter 4, speaks of God's call to the five ministry offices of the Apostle, Prophet, Pastor, Evangelist, and Teacher, in the body of Christ. Today, He is restoring and raising up those He is appointing to stand in the ministries of the Apostle and Prophet. Many today in the body of Christ are not familiar with these two ascension gifts of Jesus. Many more have believed for centuries that these offices are a thing of the past. But this is not true. For many years the ministries of Pastor, Teacher, and Evangelist have been widely accepted.

Today, we are seeing men, women, children, and youth from all walks of life and nations being transformed by the Holy Spirit and called into these much needed ministries in the body of Christ. God is using the ordinary who have a heart that is sold out to Jesus, and will continue to use them to release the mighty river of great grace that was flowing during the Book of Acts.

Upon them is the anointing of the Holy Spirit that will usher the church into greater levels of revelation, understanding, and wisdom to build His Kingdom with. Apostles and Prophets are graced in a unique way to flow together prophetically and release GREAT revelation of Jesus to the church. Their passion is to see Jesus exalted and worshipped in the house of the Lord – and to see His church healthy, in unity, maturing and advancing. As all five of these graces are restored and working together, we will see the greatest days the church has ever seen. The New Testament Church is a church that functions with all five offices in operation. As the Holy Spirit continues to restore us, we will see mind-shattering results that the earth has never seen before. In the Book of Acts, three thousand were added to their numbers daily. Imagine what your church would look like, if three thousand were added to your numbers per day.

THE AWAKENING OF
THE SLEEPING GIANT

Look Mom, in your living room, may be another Apostle like Paul, or Peter. And watch out, lining up her dolls for battle in the bedroom may be the next Prophetess, like "Deborah," who God may be raising up to lead a whole city, state, or nation back to God. God is indeed visiting the children. Calling them to deeper things of His Spirit (intercession, greater degrees of evangelism, healing, and much more). Our mouths will drop open when we see what God is going to do through our children. It's already happening in some places, and we must do our part to prepare them for all that God has instore for them.

This level of *The Mom Ministry* will require the same preliminary spiritual training for you and your children I've outlined in the beginning of this book. But will also include further equipping on the purposes and ministries of each of the five-fold offices. God wants to equip the church with His revelation so that we may be activated and released into our true callings and gifting. This is so that the lost may see Jesus, and the Bride of Christ can be fully prepared for His return.

WHY IS RECEIVING REVELATION FROM THE LORD SO IMPORTANT?

Jesus said that upon this rock (the revelation of who He is) He would build His church. He added that the gates of hell will not prevail against it. Matthew 16:15 – 19, gives us greater detail for further study. The keys of the Kingdom are these revelations that set us free from deception and bondage, and catapult us forward, causing the Kingdom of God to advance.

It was the revelation of who Jesus really is that broke the chains of deception in my life. It wasn't religion, being a good person, or even intelligence or knowledge of what is Godly that did it. It was the revelation of WHO JESUS really is. The moment He became the focus of my entire LIFE was the moment I saw Him for who He really is - - - - the TRUTH invaded every area of my heart, and changed me forever. As I began to worship HIM and focus on seeking His face, asking Him to make Himself as real to me as He did for Moses, I began to see the truth and step into the light. It was this light of revelation of who Jesus IS that dispelled the darkness in my life. He wants us to see and know Him like a true friend, like Moses, or David, Noah or Paul. God is not a respecter of persons. If you ask Him to, He will show you His glory, too!

I was transformed from a tired, broken worker, to a glorified, transformed worshipper. And upon THAT foundation, Jesus has been building ever since.

Today, the Holy Spirit is all that He was to the Acts Church. His Holy Spirit has not changed one bit, since the days of Adam, Peter, Paul, and Pentecost. He is waiting for us, as His body, to awaken and seek Him with ALL OF OUR HEARTS, LIKE THEY DID. He wants to pour out His spirit upon your household like He did then (except with even greater results).

What would happen if your entire house, or church, began to wait on God with a hungry heart like the 120 did in that upper room? Take a few minutes, read Acts Chapter 1 and 2 and ask the Holy Spirit to give you His vision and direction. Do whatever He says, no matter what it costs – and you will never be the same again (neither will your home, church, city or nation). Have you wondered why you are here and what the purpose is for you? God has a most incredible and exciting plan for your life (Jeremiah 29:11). It's far beyond your wildest and best dreams.

Revival begins with one heart repenting and giving themselves FULLY to the will and plan of God! It's not a 3-night service held at a church. It's a heart that becomes sold out to God completely. When this happens...God explodes in your life! Let it begin today in your home and in your heart. Choose to surrender all to Him! You will gain even more in return.

NOTHING CAN STOP THIS GLOBAL MOVEMENT OF THE HOLY SPIRIT

The earth has never before seen such a magnitude of His Holy movement. It's the deep waters of Ezekiel 47, multitudes of people, all ages, tongues, and tribes, are becoming dissatisfied with being a spectator on the shores of the sparkling clear water. Faithful Christians as well as unbelievers, are hungering for more of the REAL THING – the One True God and are desiring to swim in the deeper waters of His spirit. They want a REAL relationship with the REAL GOD. There's a place deep within every human being that was created for Him to fill. In this place with Him our greatest dreams and purposes are unlocked and released. No one who has ever traveled this way has been disappointed. Instead, they are deeply saddened that they did not turn to Him sooner! With every prayer and every step of obedience, Jesus is leading us and our children further out in His river of Life, to enjoy the freedom of being in HIM and over our heads in all of His goodness and love.

SPIRITUAL MOTHERING AND MENTORING

In addition to raising our children to be followers of Jesus, it's essential that we understand that God has called each woman and man of God to be mothers and fathers in the Spirit.

God's design for the church is modeled in the family. God often uses a mother or father in the Spirit to lead us to Christ – this is when we become a child of God. They are usually more mature in Christ and help us grow up to be a mother or father in the spirit, so that we can lead others to Christ – birthing more children into the Kingdom. These grow up to be mothers and fathers in the spirit…and the cycle continues. We are fruitful and multiply when we are abiding in Christ. This is the work of the Kingdom. We reproduce after our own kind.

When you are intimate with the Lord and lead someone to Christ – they become born again and like a "baby" in the Spirit. They will need loving and gentle nurturing by a more mature mother or father. As we embrace those who do not have a mentor, a phenomenon takes place. The Holy Spirit comes and fills us with spiritual milk from the Spirit and the Word of God that will feed them. As they ask questions concerning spiritual things, and we continue to pour into them, we are given more and more to feed them with.

It's revelation knowledge, imparted by the Holy Spirit through us, to feed their hungering hearts. Like a new born baby, they are hungry all the time and grow at a rapid rate of speed.

God desires to use you to mentor and encourage special ones that He will lead into your life. They will see spiritual intimacy in you that they hunger for. It will compel them to reach out to you for prayer and encouragement. God will use your life to inspire them to seek Him with all their heart.

Our role and responsibility in the Kingdom is to live the kind of life that causes a yearning inside others to draw closer to Jesus. How do we do this? By seeking Him daily with all of our hearts. Spending intimate time daily with Jesus, accomplishes miracles in minutes when we minister to the hurting. Jesus is the most deeply satisfying and glorious part of our lives. Through these moments and hours spent alone with Him, a door is opened in our lives that allows the pure and glorious light of heaven to consume us. We become radiant with HIM. We are not a mere "reflector" of Him and His light, but "full of and consumed by" HIS LIGHT. It is truly "Christ in us, the Hope of Glory." (Colossians 1:27).

Only the light of heaven can release true inspiration for the lost to come to Jesus. Those who are hungering for righteousness will be drawn into the light of Christ as you continue to abide in Him. It's this glorious light of Christ that will set the captives free and enable you to move in unity with Christ, the Head of the church.

Your role as a spiritual mother will release unlimited levels of grace and joy into your life, and theirs. Jesus took twelve and poured His Life, time, and love into their hearts. And through this work of the Holy Spirit in and through us – He desires to do the same. Mothers in the Spirit are burdened and filled with understanding, compassion, and a yearning to see the young in Christ grow in intimacy with the Lord.

In addition to your children, these "little ones" may be a Sunday School class God has blessed you with, or a young Christian whom you prayed with at the altar. Perhaps it's a struggling Mom, or a neighbor who is depressed. Perhaps your burden is for the new family that moved in two doors down or the group of teen-age girls that you see hanging out at the mall each week.

Who is God drawing your attention to? Who continues to come to your mind that you keep meaning to call? Be sensitive to the burden – pray for them. Ask the Lord to lead you to the one(s) He wants you to pour into. He'll give you scriptures for them and special words of encouragement that will spur them onward and help them overcome the many hurdles that can feel impossible in the beginning. God will use your intercession to help them break forth and be established in their calling.

Is it hard to see yourself as a Spiritual Mom? In your prayer time, ask the Lord to help you see yourself the way He does. Then choose to walk in it by faith. Then get ready for joy unspeakable.

You may be saying, "but I don't know enough." You may feel inadequate. Remember, the Holy Spirit is your helper. You can begin to share your passion for the Lord and lead others to Christ. You can listen, pray, study the word together, and continue pointing them to Jesus. Sharing what God has been doing in your family is the greatest way to mentor those who are in need. Spiritual mothering is a natural and beautiful part of the journey in the family of God. It's God's plan of multiplying the fruit of LIFE. Jesus Himself will do the work through you.

MINISTERS IN THE MARKETPLACE

The movement of God's Spirit is crossing every territorial, regional, national, generational, and marketplace line. As the church is awakening to this mighty sweep of the Lord's hand, God is calling businessmen and businesswomen into roles as marketplace apostles, prophets, evangelists, pastors, and teachers. The Spirit of God is invading the marketplace, classrooms, campuses, and church like never before. God's purpose in all of this is to completely restore and fulfill His promises and word. He will not stop until every last soul destined for His Kingdom comes in.

I'm reminded of some powerful words that the Lord spoke to my oldest son, Andrew, a few months ago. It was the night before His first day of school. He was dozing off when the Lord said to him,

"Stay close to me, so you don't miss it".

We too, must stay close to Jesus, so we don't miss what He has for us – or be found unprepared when He returns.

"...and the earth will be full of the knowledge of the Lord as the waters cover the sea."
Isaiah 11:9

If the Lord tarries, in the next 15 – 30 years it will be our children that hold some of the most influential positions in the world. Clearly this is a wake up call for Mom's (as well as the entire body of Christ) to arise and see that "it's time" for us to accept the mandate that

God is giving us. Arise and raise up our young people to be passionately, sold-out, equipped, ministers in our homes, market place, classrooms, playgrounds, and the church.   The job is too big for our church workers. The choice is ours.

It's time that we accept the call to train up our children in each of their gifts and callings. It's time to seek Him like never before, that He can remove the things in our lives that keep us bound to merely what we've been taught in the past. He will reveal the deep and hidden things that He has for our families, communities, and nation. God is doing a new thing. And it's a time of great unlocking of revelation that has been sealed up until our lifetime.

> **"He changes times and seasons;**
> **he sets up kings and deposes them.**
> **He gives wisdom to the wise**
> **and knowledge to the discerning.**
> **He reveals deep and hidden things"**
> **Daniel 2:21, 22**

Whether our children are called to write music, choreograph dances of worship to the Lord, create new things to glorify God, excel in anointed gifts of administration, or teach, it's time to seek the Lord and receive the fresh revelation that He has for our children and for this generation. It's time to make Jesus number one in our lives. We must seek Him and come up higher in the Spirit, so that we can see this generation from God's standpoint. As we do, we will be ushered into new levels of faith to speak words of life and encouragement into their lives. They are modern day Joshua's, Samuel's, Peter's, Paul's, Anna's, Esther's, Timothy's, and Deborah's…

RESOURCES AND EQUIPPING

First, we must model for them intimacy with Jesus. Second, we must do the best we can to understand and learn about their gifts and callings. Third, and most important, train them as early as possible in hearing God's voice, and knowing and studying God's Word. These are things you can begin to do today.

Teach them how to pray and listen to His voice, how to daily enter into His presence (in your home). Teaching them that He speaks to us with the still small voice in their heart, and loves them unconditionally. Teach them the importance of keeping a pure heart, and how important it is to cry out to God for His Kingdom to come and His will to be done in the earth today.

He will lead you to the right resources and training He wants you to have for them. Daily, in our homes, we can have personal classroom sessions with the Holy Spirit, our Teacher. And it's thrilling to grow to KNOW Him more together, with our family.

"I pray also that the eyes of your heart may be enlightened in order that you may know the hope to which he has called you, the riches of his glorious inheritance in the saints, and his incomparably great power for us who believe. That power is like the working of his mighty strength, which he exerted in Christ when he raised him from the dead and seated him at his right hand in the heavenly realms..."
Ephesians 1:17-20

Ask God for wisdom, revelation, and insight into the future ministries that He has planned for your children. Whether their ministries are in the home, church, or marketplace. Pray Ephesians 1:17, 18 often for them, and record in your *Mom Ministry Journal* the revelations and insights He gives you. As God begins to show you and confirm glimpses of His callings and gifts for them, pray in agreement with His word and what He's showing you.

JOURNALING

Your journal will serve as a valuable documentary and written record of your path of revelation and miracles. There will be much to praise the Lord for! A log for the miracles, signs, and wonders that are going to increase in your lives. It will serve as a record of answered prayers, and breakthroughs in your marriage and family. Later, your journal can serve as a special gift to them, or even a weapon against the enemy when He comes to make you doubt that your children will fulfill the call and purpose that God has for each of their lives.

WHY TEACH THEM TO JOURNAL, NOW?

Why is it so helpful to teach our children early to journal? I believe, it is one of the easiest ways to help teach a child how to hear the voice of God. As they pray, it can be used to train them to be still and wait on the Lord for a golden nugget from His throne. It instills in them the value in waiting for one precious thought from His heart to ours. It implants in their hearts and mind that they are so precious and special to God that He's waiting to fill the heart that is yearning to hear from Him. It can help make God so REAL to them. When they are older, their journals will be priceless to them and their children.

The Lord often speaks to us in smaller parts, and when recorded in writing, flow together to give us a bigger and fuller revelation of what He is saying. As we hold it to the light of the Word, the Holy Spirit will magnify and illuminate scripture to you. The world is teaching our children to journal ~ why not teach them to not only hear from Him, but to journal what they hear from the Creator of all the universe.

Even one word that we hear in the spirit over and over, can mean something huge. It can be the key to unlock a huge and mighty message or revelation from God. Teaching them to take our messages to prayer, how to use the concordance, how to look up key words in the dictionary, helps them to learn how to "dig for the finest of pearls" in God's word.

You can help them record any dreams or visions they may have. Do so by encouraging them to record as many details as possible without adding to or taking away from what they actually heard, saw, sensed or experienced. Then look-up key words in scripture and discover what the Holy Spirit is revealing to you.

This also teaches them how to see more in the Spirit and trains them to seek God for the interpretation, like Daniel did. God uses all of these things to affirm and establish them in their faith and in the joys of hearing the Lord's voice and knowing Him.

For further study on how to train up children in the prophetic, study also Eli and how He taught Samuel to hear and recognize God's voice. This is a priceless thing to instill in the hearts of your children.

ARE MY CHILDREN PROPHETIC?

Children that are sensitive to the Holy Spirit, often times are visionary or may speak words that inspire people toward the heart of Jesus. AJ, my youngest, received His first night vision (a vision in the night), at the age of 3. He has had many dreams about Jesus. Children all over the world, today, are being visited by God. You may have already noticed this in your own home.

It's important to record and save them if possible, as they are literally messages from God. They are not to be taken lightly. We record them as accurately as possible (I did it for AJ until He could learn to write). God often uses them to reveal specific things to our hearts, and confirm things to us. God uses them to draw us closer to Him and assure us of His great power and control in our lives.

After prayer, If a message in a dream, vision, or teaching, does not line up with scripture, we do not receive it. Those that are scriptural, but are not understood, are saved for a later time. The Bible says that it is by two or more witnesses (or confirmations) that we receive words from the Lord. Meaning: God will always confirm His will and word for us.

Prophetic messages are never to be used as a replacement for God's word. They are messages that confirm the truth and His Word in our lives. Aligning them with the word and teaching our children to spend quality time in prayer is essential. Prophetic messages are intended to draw us closer to the Lord and help keep us centered in His will for our lives.

TRUE PROPHECY

Being prophetic is not spooky nor is it something to brag about. It also does not necessarily mean that one is a "prophet". Prophetic Ministry is a wonderful and powerful ministry but is not in itself to be the focus. The focus of true prophetic ministry is Jesus. God's word describes true prophecy in Revelation 19:10:

**"...Worship God! For the testimony of Jesus
is the spirit of prophecy."**

Prophetic messages are a normal, healthy function of the New and Old Testament Church. Jesus spoke prophetically all the time. He spoke what He heard the Father saying, and did what He saw the Father doing. The Acts church is a prophetic church, led by the Holy Spirit's voice, confirmation, and guidance. Paul speaks of it extensively in His writings. Moses wished that all could prophesy. Yet, the focus must always remain on the King of Kings and Lord of Lord's Himself. The gifts and manifestations in the spirit are to point and align our paths to intimacy with Jesus, and a right relationship with God our Father. God also gives us direction prophetically, to direct us in the way that we should go.

Does it mean we should never speak of or teach on prophetic ministry, or about the gifts of the spirit? No. Training is necessary so that we may understand and grow in maturity. Paul did many teachings regarding prophecy in the church. It was necessary because there was so much of it flowing in the church, they needed to prevent services from being filled with disorder and chaos.

But without quenching the spirit, we are to be careful to keep the focus of prophecies on target. The gifts are given to the church to point us to the Way, the Truth, and the Life, Himself - Jesus. The Book of Acts is an excellent textbook for the gifts of the spirit operating in the church today. The Holy Spirit's voice speaking to His church, gives us direction, correction, and/or protection. In Him alone is found truth, life, and the only way to our Loving Father.

How can you tell the difference between the True and the Counterfeit? One way is to recognize the following:

- The Counterfeit Prophetic will glorify the gift.
- The True Prophetic ministry will glorify the "giver" of the gift.

True prophetic people, are intimate with Jesus, study His Word, love to pray, intercede, worship, draw closer to God, and insist upon pointing people to the Lord. They often times will sense something, hear something from the Lord, and receive direction from the Holy Spirit. They are open vessels, filled with His spirit, and able to flow in Him, bringing unity, His love, and restoration to those who are open to receive more of Jesus.

IT'S ALL ABOUT HIM!

All of God's people walk in the Spirit. Paul wrote in Romans 8:14, "...*because those who are led by the Spirit of God are sons of God.*"

I've learned it's not about goose bumps, the gifts of the Spirit, healing, and being mesmerized by the power of God, but it's all about God our Father, Jesus His son, and the Holy Spirit, and having an intimate relationship with Him (every day). I praise God for each of these manifestations of His spirit. They are necessary in the body and are given as gifts to us by the Lord, that we may know Him more, prosper, and be healthy in our mind, soul, and spirit.

We are very aware that the Spirit of Jesus dwells not only in our hearts, but rests upon our home. Those who are intimate with Him, understand that we are enveloped by Him. Walking IN His Spirit. What a precious gift we have – to know that He is real and the center of our lives. There was a sad time, when Jesus was nothing more to us than a picture of the man who lived long ago. All we knew was "religion" (man working in His own strength to reach God) and we tried so hard to reach Him and look for peace and satisfaction. We looked in all the wrong places. Thank God for the day He opened our eyes to the fact that He is here – He is "Emmanuel", "God WITH us". God is more real to us than what we see with our eyes.

It seems that many are curious about this passion for Jesus and how it is that we say we can hear Him speak, and sense His presence. To tell you the truth, there are also some churched people that have a difficult time understanding this kind of relationship we have with Him. This is our testimony about what God has done in our home, marriage, and life!

God is restoring His Acts Church! It's His design and His time. I'm so glad He moved us out of our comfort zone to seek Him with all of our hearts. Inside of us grew a desire for more of Him than ever before. And we never want to go back. In Him, we've found everything our hearts have ever searched for – and more. What a blessing and privilege it is to be a part of God's plan!

ARE YOU READY?

We discovered something as we've journeyed this exciting path with God - He'll give you more, and more and more of His heart. This journey with Him is certainly about discovering MORE OF HIM, every day. In HIM, there IS more - - more than we can imagine. What He did in the Book of Acts was only the beginning of His last days outpouring – and it included a place for the whole family. Our "sons and daughters", too! The best is yet to come for our families. God desires all of us to be a part of what He's doing.

We've got an exciting job ahead of us, Moms. Discovering our life's assignment, and deeper levels of Him, with our children, is the most thrilling experience in the world. Preparing them for their life's work in the Kingdom of God is part of God's thrilling plan for us. It's far better than going through life, just trying to make it through the day. We are training them to reign with Christ! What we sow in them, will be reaped for eternity!

He's pouring out His Spirit upon every man, woman, boy and girl today that will seek Him whole-heartedly. He's revealing Himself to man through dreams, visions, and showing signs and wonders in the heavens above and the earth below - just like He said He would! He's looking for Mom's, Dad's, children, sisters, brothers, and families, that will open their hearts and lives to Him and surrender saying, "Come Lord, sit on the throne of our lives. Take your rightful place in us – glorify yourself through us, Lord, we want MORE of YOU!"

Oh Lord,

I pray for our eyes ~ to see what You see.
Lord, that we would have ears to hear what you are
saying to the church, and to our families.
Lord, that we would carry Your Heart,
touch with Your hands,
and go in your spirit and power.

I pray that your Spirit will flow...
YES, LORD – Restore us, and build our families,
our children, and your church through us.
Enable us, by your Spirit to prepare the way for YOU.
Jesus...we want to be
ready, waiting, and looking for You ~
You are Our Lord, Savior, Healer, Deliverer, Redeemer,
and BEST FRIEND!

Thank You, Jesus – for everything!
To YOU be all the Honor and Glory
Forever and Ever!
The Spirit and the Bride say, "Come, Lord Jesus, Come."

**"The Spirit and the bride say, "Come!"
and let him who hears say, "Come!" Whoever
is thirsty, let him come; and whoever wishes, let him
take the free gift of the water of life."
Revelation 22:17**

Resources & Equipping

Wagner Leadership Institute
C. Peter Wager
Colorado Springs, CO
Website:
www.wagnerleadership.org
Phone: 800-683-9630

Christian International Ministries
Dr. Bill Hamon
Santa Rosa Beach, FL
Website:
www.christianinternational.org
Phone: 800-388-5308

Crusaders Ministries
Apostle John Eckhardt
Matteson, IL
Phone: 708-922-0983

Kids in Ministry International, Inc.
- Kids
Becky Fischer
Bismarck, ND
Website: www.kidsinministry.com
Phone: 701-258-6786

Superkidz 4 Christ
- Kids
Robb & Jacqui Dunham
Atascadero, CA
Website:
www.superkidz4christ.com

Karen Wheaton Ministries
– Teens / Young Adults
Chosen Generation / "The Ramp"
Hamilton, AL
Website: www.karenwheaton.com
Phone: 1-800-345-2736

Focus on the Family
- Family
Dr. James Dobson
Colorado Springs, Colorado 80920
Website: www.family.org
Phone: 719-531-3400

Children's Ministries Agency
General Council of the Assemblies
of God
Springfield, MO 65802
Website: www.4kids.ag.org
Phone: 417-862-2781 (ext. 4009)

More Recommended Resources

Praying God's Word, by Beth Moore
The Voice of God, by Cindy Jacobs
Me and My Big Mouth, by Joyce Meyers
There Were Two Trees In the Garden, by Rick Joyner
The Grace Awakening, by Charles Swindoll,
I Give You Authority, by Charles H. Kraft
The Gifts & Ministries of the Holy Spirit, by Lester Sumrall
Good Morning Holy Spirit, by Benny Hinn
The Vision, by Rick Joyner
Prophet's Dictionary, by Paula A. Price, Ph.D.
God's Timing for Your Life, by Dutch Sheets
Thus Saith the Lord? by John Bevere
A Woman's Guide to Spiritual Warfare, by
        Quin Sherrer & Ruthanne Garlock
Deliverance for Children & Teens, by Bill Banks
Strongman's His Name What's His Game?
        By Drs. Jerry & Carol Robeson
The Three Battlegrounds, by Francis Frangipane
Ridding Your Home of Spiritual Darkness, by Chuck Pierce
Breaking Intimidation, by John Bevere
They Shall Expel Demons, by Derek Prince
The Pursuit of God, by A. W. Tozer
Beyond The Veil, by Alice Smith
Intimate Friendship with God, by Joy Dawson
Intercessory Prayer, by Dutch Sheets
Prayer, A Holy Occupation, by Oswald Chambers
Too Busy Not to Pray, by Bill Hybels

CHILDREN'S WORSHIP ALBUMS –

"Historymaker", (Worship for Kids), available at
www.Superkidz4Christ.com
"Superkidz Sing with a Heart of Worship", available at
www.Superkidz4Christ.com

CHILDREN –

Children of Revival, by Vann Lane

TO CONTACT US

"We want to hear from you!"

Please contact us with your **prayer requests**,
testimonies of how your life has been touched,
or **inquiries,** at the following addresses:

EMAIL ~ themomministry@ignite-ministries.org
WEBSITE ~ www.ignite-ministries.org
MAILING ADDRESS ~ IGNITE Ministries
    P.O. BOX 132, Crystal Lake, IL 60039-0132
OFFICE PHONE ~ 815. 788.8178

Andy and Lisa Hartell founded *IGNITE Ministries* in response to
God's call to equip the body of Christ,
and reach the lost with the good news of His Kingdom,
both locally and internationally.

To purchase additional copies of this book,
please visit our website, or use the enclosed order form.

"The Mom Ministry" Order Form

Use this convenient order form to order by mail,
or visit our website to order on-line:
www.ignite-ministries.org

Please Print:

Name: _____

Address: _____

City: _____ State: _____

Zip: _____

Phone: (   ) _____

_____ copies of book @ 12.99 each $ _____
Shipping & Handling @ $2.50 per book $ _____
Total amount enclosed $ _____

For larger quantities, call ahead for shipping price.
815.788.8178

Make checks payable to:
        "Lisa Hartell / Ignite Ministries"

Send To: IGNITE Ministries
                P.O. Box 132, Crystal Lake, IL 60039-0132

ENDNOTES

Chapter ONE ~
[i] "More Than Conquerors", p. 183, by John Woodbridge, 1992 Moody Press.

Chapter TWO ~
[ii] "The American Heritage Dictionary", Second College Edition, 1982, Houghton Mifflin Company.

Chapter THREE ~
[iii] "The American Heritage Dictionary", Second College Edition, 1982, Houghton Mifflin Company.

Chapter THREE ~
[iv] "The Prophet's Dictionary", by Paula A. Price, Ph.D., 1999, Flaming Vision Publications.

Chapter NINE ~
[v] "The Healing Anointing", by Kenneth E. Hagin, 1997, Faith Library Publications.

Chapter TEN ~
[vi] "I Give You Authority", by Charles H. Kraft, 1997, Chosen Books.